GREEK VASES

To my parents,

to Jean, Isabelle, Jacques & Co.

FRANÇOIS LISSARRAGUE

GREEK VASES

THE ATHENIANS AND THEIR IMAGES

RIVERSIDE BOOK COMPANY, INC.

Acknowledgments

To Eric Hazan, without whom this book would not have existed, and to all those who have supported its development, in particular Eric Reinhardt, Juliette Hazan and Valerie Graftieaux.

To Antoine Hazan, impeccable editor, and to Françoise Frontisi-Ducroux, for their patient reading and critical eye (the errors which remain are evidently my own).

To Stefano Bianchetti, who explained to me the tricks of lighting.

To Michel Bats, who knows how to work miracles in Naples, and to Ludi Chazalon who opened the doors of Sing-Sing to me.

And finally to Gratianne, who pressured me at the right moment.

Without free access to the vases, this book would have been impossible: therefore, great thanks to those curators and museum officials who have generously accommodated me over the years. In particular, for the realization of this book, Robert Guy and Michael Padgett in Princeton, Angelo Bottinni and Anna Rastrelli in Florence, Stefano de Caro in Naples and Martine Denoyelle in the Louvre, and finally and especially Irène Aghion in the Cabinet des Médailles of the Bibliothèque Nationale, whose help, once again, proved irreplaceable.

TABLE OF CONTENTS

F O R E W O R D

This book is a miscellany, an anthology, a bouquet of images. There exist in our day thousands of Greek vases, exhibited in or in storage at museums in Europe and America, before which the visitor often passes hastily; such an abundance of pottery can sometimes be discouraging.

The vases are fragile but the shards are almost indestructible and considerable quantities of more or less intact ceramics have been preserved. They bring joy to archaeologists: indelible traces of a distant past, the broken pots pay and reward the digger for his meticulousness. Indications of a presence, clues for a dating, the vases contribute to the writing of history.

All ancient cultures produced pottery; among them, Greek ceramics distinguish themselves by their quality and the particular nature of their decoration, which establishes their connection to painting. The Greeks elaborated a type of decoration centered on the human figure very early on. From the geometric in the 8th century BC and the motifs which give their name to this style (meanders, circles, chevrons, etc.), one sees the image of man appear, in combat or at the time of funerals. The so-called Orientalising style, in the 7th Century, moves away for a time from these types of subjects, favoring animal and floral decoration. As Athens asserted itself in the Mediterranean world at the end of the 7th century BC, it revived a type of pottery founded on a technique of black figures (the black silhouettes stand out on a background of red clay), and then, in the 5th century, one of red figures (they are left unpainted, or reserved, on a background of black glaze). This Attic production alone has left us more than 80,000 vases.

A choice must be made. The plan of action here is not to follow the typology of the vases nor the history of the painters and artisans in their chronological development, questions with which others have already dealt in depth elsewhere and which are indicated here in the appendix. The choice, centered more upon the representations than on the pottery, is thematic. The aesthetic quality of the works is important, but this book does not limit itself only to masterpieces, to the great classics of the Greek vase. Alongside the major pieces (particularly those attributed to the so-called Kleophrades painter, to whom we credit the cover of this book, with seven vases distributed among six chapters) appear objects which are less well-known, including fragments whose importance is not inconsiderable and which draw our attention to certain aspects of the culture and beliefs of the Athenians.

The following chapters are organized beginning with the banquet, where the vases were especially used; from there one moves to erotic relationships, then to other forms of social life where the dominant masculine identity defines itself: athletic and musical competitions, war and its heroic role models. The rites of passage, of weddings, and of funerals open upon the religious aspects of life and their representation, which give the vases an important ritual role. Then comes the representation of the sacrifice, which sets up the relationship between men and gods. Finally, the mythical dimension of Greek culture is addressed, with Herakles, the hero above all heroes; then other specifically Athenian myths, before coming to Dionysos, whose place on drinking vases is essential. This route is framed, by way of prologue and epilogue, with an analysis of two particularly rich and complex kraters: the "François Vase" in the opening, dating from around 570 BC, and in the closing, the "Krater of Pronomos," from the 410's BC; situated at the chronological limits of the period discussed here (essentially the 6th and 5th centuries BC in Athens), these two vases allow us to concretely introduce the question of image and its medium, its material and cultural context.

This anthology, composed to please the eye, seeks to make perceptible and intelligible these objects which were not made to illustrate Athenian life but which convey the visual way of thinking and experiencing through which many aspects of this society were aestheticized, as though the painters held a mirror to the Athenians themselves.

PROLOGUE

1. *Beilage zur Allgemeine Zeitung,* June 22 1845, p. 1379

On November 3, 1844, Alessandro François, "an enterprising and active man to whom archaeology owes a great deal,"[1] pursuing the exploration of the necropolis of Chiusi, excavated the surroundings of an important tumulus. In the access corridor to the funeral chamber, he collected the first piece of an Attic krater; other numerous fragments were found in a passage dug out in antiquity by pillagers who came to divest the dead of their subterranean riches.

Struck by the quality of this vase, Alessandro François lost no time in seeking to convert its value into cash. On December 14, 1844, he informed the Director of the Galleries of Florence by letter that: "I have recently discovered below the lands of Chiusi many interesting objects...and in particular a magnificent vase, whose equal I have never seen; even though it is missing a few pieces, it was found sufficiently remarkable for me to be offered one hundred ten [gold] sequins, which I believe to be less than its value..."

Other fragments were found in April 1845; the vase was finally purchased for five hundred sequins by the Grand Duke of Tuscany on August 30, 1845 and delivered to the Uffizzi. When Alessandro François died in October 1857, he had not abandoned resuming his excavations to find the missing pieces. In fact, an isolated fragment was offered to the museum in 1861, in exchange for a job; but the management refused such bargaining and this piece rejoined the vase only after having changed owners. It was given to the museum by Carlo Strozzi in 1866.

This vase, which very quickly became famous under the name of its finder, the François Vase, constituted for a long time, in spite of its fragmented state, one of the jewels of the Archaeological Museum of Florence. This fame probably earned it its final transformation: on September 9, 1900, a museum employee, overcome with rage, after

▶ 1. BLACK-FIGURE KRATER, SIDE A. SIGNED KLEITIAS AND ERGOTIMOS. 580 BC. HT. 0.66M. ARCHAEOLOGICAL MUSEUM, FLORENCE.

► 4. SIDE B OF THE VASE

2, 3. VIEWS OF THE HANDLES

having wounded a museum guard with a knife, seized a heavy stool and broke the display case, along with the vase which it protected. The krater was then entirely restored in 1902. It was restored again in 1973, then cleared of some repaints which sought to partially hide any gaps in the decoration. It is not impossible that still more fragments will be found: archaeology is done in this manner, in bits and pieces.

The symbolic importance of this object involves more than its anecdotal value. It has to do with one of the most important monuments of archaic Greek art, introduced in Etruria as an object of prestige to decorate the dwelling, and then the tomb, of a local aristocrat. The artisans who crafted it around 570 BC, the potter Ergotimos and the painter Kleitias, legitimately proud of their work, each signed his name.

This vase has medium-sized dimensions: with its 66 centimeters in height and 57 centimeters in diameter, it is far from achieving the size of the great geometric kraters of the 8th century or of those made in southern Italy in the 4th century. It has, nevertheless, a monumental character, owing to the richness and complexity of its decoration, which the miniaturist style with which the figures are created – they do not exceed 8cm – makes dense and precious at the same time. The minuteness of the delicately incised details is often more reminiscent of the work of the engraver and goldsmith than that of the sculptor. But the general volume of this krater is treated as a sort of architecture, with a series of friezes which follow the articulations of the neck, belly and foot. The large flat handles which rise into a curl from the grips which form the handles are also decorated with figures. The entire vase is composed of six superimposed friezes, two on the neck, three on the belly, and one on the foot: in total over 159 characters appear, accompanied by 130 inscriptions which allow us to name them and to grasp that which is essential in the themes represented.

It is not a question of entering here into a minutely detailed description of all these scenes, but a quick skimming of the whole of this imagery allows a concrete assessment of the richness of the archaic repertoire and of the way in which Kleitias, the painter, has associated different mythical themes. The François vase has sometimes been likened to a sort of poetic bible, or a Greek comic strip. Neither of these metaphors, which are too marked by our culture of writing, really accounts for the way in which the image proceeds, by association and by accumulation.

2. Pindar, *Isthmian Odes,* VIII 35-40.

The main frieze, at the top of the belly, is both the tallest and the only one – along with the one which decorates the foot – to make a complete rotation around the vase. On it one sees a long parade of chariots, an impressive procession which advances from left to right, towards the residence of Thetis, daughter of Nereus and Doris, divinities of the sea.

Pindar recalls the story of the wedding of Thetis and Peleus. An oracle of Themis announced to the gods "that the sea goddess would bring into the world a son who would become a leader stronger than his father and whose hand would send flying a shot more fearsome than lightning or the monstrous trident if she were to marry Zeus or one of the brothers of Zeus. If you obey me," Themis continues "you will grant to Peleus the son of Aeacos the honor of this marriage which will ally him to the gods." [2] And so Peleus, with the help of the centaur Chiron, won the hand of Thetis, against her will. On the François vase, she is seated inside her house, partially hidden by the flap of a double door, lifting her veil to receive the cortege which has come to greet her and her new husband. Peleus stands upright outside the house, turned towards the gods who approach. He grasps the hand of the centaur Chiron, above the domestic altar. The signature of Kleitias extends itself, vertically, between the joined hands of the two accomplices and the altar upon which stands a kantharos. Iris, messenger of the gods, carrier of the caduceus, leads the way with Chiron who is weighed down with game. Coming next, in close rank, are three goddesses side by side – Demeter, Hestia, and Chariklo. Then comes Dionysos, who brings on his shoulder a large amphora and turns his face to the front, towards the viewer of the vase. He is followed by the Three Horai, the Seasons, next to which one reads, vertically, the signature of the potter, Ergotimos. Then begins the long parade of chariots, driven by the gods and accompanied by figures who walk at their sides. Zeus and Hera are first, with the Muses, Ourania and Kalliope, who also faces front like Dionysos, playing the *syrinx*. Then, partially hidden by the handle, Poseidon and Amphitrite; their silhouettes are not seen, but their names inscribed suffice in making them present. With them, four Muses: Melpomene, Kleio, Euterpe, and Thaleia. Under the handle, also hidden but present by name, are Ares and Aphrodite, with three Muses: Stesichore, Erato and Polyhymnia. The next chariot, quite incomplete, remains anonymous to us (perhaps one would find there Apollo and Artemis, or Leto, with the Charites). Athena and a goddess in a chariot follow, accompanied by Nereus and Doris on foot. Then Hermes and Maia, his mother, with the Moirai. Finally, a last chariot, of which only a trace survives. Under the handle, to loop the circle around the belly, the god with the body of a fish, Okeanos, marks the end of the parade as the limit of the inhabited world; he is in the company of Hephaistos, misshapen, on his mule, bringing up the rear, the true outcast of Olympus.

In total, seven chariots making the march of a series of gods who are not normally joined as matrimonial couples, and the groups of secondary female divinities, presented collectively: the Horai, the Muses, perhaps the Graces, and the Moirai. All the energies which preside over the proper functioning of the human world, over the unfolding of yearly or biological time, as well as the major forces to which the world is subject, solemnly come to pay a visit to the newly established couple Thetis and Peleus, as if to guarantee by their presence the prosperity of this half-divine, half-human couple who will give birth to the most famous of all Greek heroes, Achilles.

Peleus is also found in the highest band of the neck. This frieze, framed on both ends by two sphinxes and vertical bands of floral embellishments, is organized symmetrically around an enormous wild boar which a series of hunters confront with their pikes. In the first row, facing the animal, Peleus stands next to Meleager; behind them Atalanta, the beautiful hunter, and Melanion, the one who could be called the "black hunter." Castor and Pollux, the divine twins, attack the animal from behind in order to free Antaios who is lodged beneath the wild boar. In total, nineteen hunters unite to collectively come against the enormous animal sent by Artemis to ravage the region of Calydon. This hunting by Meleager, in which Peleus plays an important role, is an example of the quasi-initiatory value of this exercise, marking the passage of a young man to the stage of accomplished warrior.

On the lower register a chariot race takes place; five harnesses are launched in a manner which is a bit rigid and repetitive. Under the legs of the horses are a cauldron and a tripod; these are the prizes reserved for the winners. At the extreme left of the frieze, upright, immobile near the tripod, stands Achilles, staff in hand, judging the race. The frieze thus represents the games that the son of Peleus organized at the time of the funeral of Patroklos, games to which Book XXIII of the *Iliad* is entirely dedicated. But Kleitias does not trouble himself with following Homer to the letter. Here it is Odysseus who leads, whereas he is only a spectator in the *Iliad*. He is followed by

Automedon and Diomedes; the winner of the event in Homer is third here. Damasippos and Hippothoon, also near the marker at the end of the track, are unknown to the poet. The image is not the illustration of the text as we know it, but there is no good reason to charge Kleitias with ignorance: he represents in his own way a story well-known by contemporary viewers.

Achilles is again the principal hero of the frieze which runs below the cortege of gods. The scene occupies one whole side of the vase, and spreads out from one structure to another. To the left is a fountain with its columns and its architrave, named *krene*, or "fountain," in an inscription: it does not have to do with facilitating an obvious identification, but with giving to this building a status equal to that of a person. The fountain is the key place in the episode portrayed; not just a simple decoration, but a point of articulation in the story. Apollo stands upright at the side of the building; a young Trojan *(Troon)* comes there to refill his hydria, along with, perhaps, the young Rhodia, standing on raised ground to the right of the fountain. Thetis, the mother of Achilles, Hermes and Athena witness the scene, which, unfortunately for us, is fragmentary (but known because of other vases). Achilles rushes forward in pursuit of the young Trojan prince, Troilos, who has come to water his horses. Polyxene, the sister of Troilos, panic-stricken, has dropped her vase (labelled *hydria*). Further on the right, Antenor goes and alerts King Priam, who is sitting on a chair *(thakos)* in front of the ramparts of Troy. The reinforcements prepare to come to the help of Troilos: through the open door of the city one sees Polites (the Townsman) and Hektor, the oldest brother of Troilos, coming out with their weapons, Hektor's shield decorated with the monstrous face of the Gorgon. Between the fountain and the rampart the entire drama of Troilos is evoked along with the savage violence of Achilles in ambush, ready to do harm to the young imprudent adolescents who have come out of the city.

The next register on this side does not recall any particular mythological episode. It is symmetrically constructed around a complex floral element flanked by two immobile sphinxes; the same which frame the hunt of the Calydonian boar in the uppermost frieze. Then come pairs of savage animals: to the left a panther devours a hart; to the right another panther attacks a bull. Such motifs, which fit within an Oriental and Corinthian tradition, are particularly elaborate here: these animal battles evoke the metaphors which in the epic are used to indicate the strength and valor of the heroes.

8. DETAIL OF THE FOOT

The last register is the frieze which decorates the foot of the vase. There exists no other example of its ornamental type in Attic ceramics; the foot is generally only a minor area of the vase and while the potters often sought to change the shape of it, the painters never intervened in this area. Kleitias and Ergotimos give here still more proof of their originality. The frieze runs all around the vase, without cessation, with the exception of the modern gaps. One sees here an

9. DETAIL OF THE HANDLE

immense battle of miniature men against long-legged birds with their wings spread wide. The motif of the combat of the Pygmies and the cranes is known from the *Iliad,* which alludes to it in comparing the clamor of warriors launching into battle with that of the Pygmies frightened by the birds. These Pygmies are of small stature – their name means "cubit" – but they are not at all deformed or ridiculous, and the humor one perceives in this hunt, which parodies at the same time both epic war and the heroic hunt, is neither caricatured nor grotesque. The scene is an echo, in an amusing way, of the hunt of the wild boar of Calydon, higher up on the vase; we are here at the other end of the world, in a mythical and far away land, but also at the end of a vase whose surface, including the foot, is treated as a microcosm.

Moving to the other side of the krater, one is struck by the decoration of the handles which repeats itself with a few variations on each one. The large, tall surface of the curled handles is divided into three nearly square panels, in the style of metopes. Towards the interior of the bowl are two running Gorgons while on the outside a goddess occupies the upper panel. Upright, with immobile wings outspread, she holds in each hand a wild animal, adopting here the appearance of Artemis the huntress, "mistress of the animals" *(potnia theron).* From one handle to the other, the bestiary changes; two lions on one side, a panther and hart on the other: these are variations similar to those noted on the frieze of palmettes and animals on the lower belly.

Under the goddess, as if to confirm the dominant theme of the principal surface, the dead Achilles is carried away from the battlefield by Ajax. The hero is naked, without arms or armor, his body dangling over the shoulder of Ajax, his hair undone and hanging down in long uniform locks. Nothing is repulsive about this image of a cadaver: Achilles is beautiful in his eternal glory.

Although the main surface seems relatively homogenous, since one sees there all around and from top to bottom Peleus in the hunt of the

9. DETAIL OF THE HANDLE

10. DETAIL OF THE NECK, SIDE B, UPPERMOST REGISTER

11. DETAIL OF THE NECK, SIDE B, UPPERMOST REGISTER

Calydonian boar, as well as Achilles and the Games for Patroklos, the wedding of Thetis and Peleus, and finally Achilles pursuing Troilos, the different registers on the other side are more thematically varied.

The upper frieze is defaced on the left; one is able to see there the trace of a double signature, repeating the names of Kleitias and Ergotimos, above a long ship with a great and animated crew. To the right, seven young boys and seven young girls in alternation hold hands in a long farandole led by Theseus, who advances, lyre in hand, towards Ariadne and her nurse. After having freed them from the Minotaur, Theseus leads the young Athenians; it is the moment of liberation, perhaps the one in which Theseus, landing in Delos, invents a dance called the *geranos,* the dance of the crane, which verbally echoes the scene on the foot of the vase.

On the next register, also defaced, Theseus appears again; at the extreme left of the frieze, his name survives between two gaps. The battle is raging between five groups of Lapiths and centaurs. The latter are armed with trees and rocks; a few bear names which emphasize their violence or their rustic character: Hylaios (the Forester), Petraios (Rocky), Agrios (the Savage). Facing them, the Lapiths, armed as hoplites – one of them is called Hoplon – energetically resist. The presence of Theseus implies that this combat took place during the wedding of Peirithoos and Hippodamaia. The drunken centaurs attempted to capture the bride and rape her, which is bad manners. Just above the frieze where the gods parade in good order to acclaim the wedding of Thetis and Peleus, the scene offers in its disorder a striking contrast. The two models are opposed by juxtaposition: the society of the Olympian gods and the savagery of the centaurs, between human and animal.

Below this procession of gods, which we have seen makes a complete turn around the vase, one moves from the world of heroes,· Achilles or Theseus, to that of the Olympians. The scene is not

12. DETAIL OF THE BELLY, SIDE B, LOWER REGISTER

constructed in a linear fashion, from left to right, as are most of the preceding scenes, but according to a convergent scheme, as in the hunt of the Calydonian boar. To the left is an assembly of gods, behind the throned Zeus. His wife Hera is also seated upon a throne; then come Athena, Ares, Artemis, and then undoubtedly Poseidon and Hermes. Before these seven gods a cortege advances, received by Aphrodite. Dionysos leads a mule upon which is seated Hephaistos. A band of Sileni and nymphs bring up the rear. It is the return of Hephaistos to Olympia. The lame, deformed god was banished from the heavens by his mother Hera. Welcomed by Thetis, he pretends to reconcile himself with his mother and offers her a throne which is in fact a trap: once seated, she cannot stand. To free her from it, the help of Hephaistos is needed. Ares is first to try in vain to bring him back to Hera; only Dionysos succeeds, by making him drink. The power of wine weakened the resolve of this blacksmith god and triumphs over his trickery. Through the power of wine which loosens the limbs, Dionysos gains the upper hand over the metal which forges chains. Hephaistos returns among his own, the Olympians; in finally freeing his mother, he finds again his place next to his wife Aphrodite. At the same time, in thanks, Dionysos also gains his definitive place among the gods. The wine serves to confirm the status of these gods as members of the Greek pantheon.

The position of Dionysos on the François vase is noteworthy. He appears twice, each time leading a procession: either that of the gods visiting Peleus, in which he carries an amphora as a gift, or that of Hephaistos, in which it is the satyrs who carry a wineskin. One must remember here what a krater is: a vase for mixing wine which, placed at the center of the banquet room, is also the center of attention. The importance given to wine on these two friezes is perfectly appropriate for the function of the krater.

The main frieze of this complex vase recalls the power of the Olympian gods and their special alliance with Peleus. The place occupied by Dionysos and Hephaistos, at the head and the rear of the cortege, is commented upon in the lower register in the scene of the reintegration of the outcast gods in Olympus. The rest of the vase treats heroic motifs from a specific viewpoint; not the epic combats where heroes clash on the battlefield, but the casual episodes: the collective hunt; funeral games; an ambush which highlights the exploits of Peleus or Achilles; a battle against the savage world; Minotaurs and centaurs, with Theseus, the Athenian hero par excellence; and combat against the cranes, at the end of the world, on the side of the Pygmies.

The ensemble of these images does not confine itself to one cycle or one strictly constructed program, but plays upon the more subtle coherences made from thematic or formal associations. The advance of the chariots, for example, is echoed by Troilos' horse hunt; the architecture of the home of Thetis is matched by that of the walls of Troy. These formal equivalents pair with the thematic equivalents – the exploits of Peleus, Achilles, and Theseus – which enrich each other by juxtaposition. In this sense, the iconographic program of the François vase functions like the poetry sung at the banquet. It leans upon the poetic memory and shared knowledge which make up archaic culture. The image evokes the themes and episodes which the viewer knows and which he is able to recite orally. Not one of the thematic connections made by Kleitias on this vase is signalled in advance, but each motif gains in substance by contact with the others. The juxtaposition, for example, of the cortege of the gods at the marriage of Peleus with the pitched battle at the wedding of Peirithoos makes more evident the contrast between order and disorder which characterizes these episodes. Pindar proceeds similarly in his odes; in the third *Pythian Ode* he evokes in parallel the weddings of Peleus and Kadmos, and each story enriches itself in the meaning of the other.

Such a thematic field is relatively limited in its archaic repertoire, but the possible combinations are quite vast. This is precisely what makes for the richness of the archaic figurative repertoire and of archaic poetry, which find their privileged place of expression on the vases and at the banquet.

AT THE BANQUET 1

► 14. ATTIC RED-FIGURE PLATE, SIGNED EPICTETOS
520 BC, DIAMETER 0.19 M
PARIS, CABINET DES MÉDAILLES, BIBLIOTHÈQUE NATIONALE

Dionysos gave to man the gifts of wine and the vine. It is up to man to make good use of them. The first drinkers, those in the time of Icarios, the peasant from Attica who was the first to receive that god come from afar, learned this at their own expense. In parting, to thank him for his welcome, Dionysos left a wineskin. When Icarios served this drink to the neighboring shepherds, they became drunk and behaved like lunatics, unable to tolerate the strength of the beverage. They thought themselves poisoned and killed the peasant. When Erigone discovered the dead body of her father, she hanged herself in despair. Dionysos, who knew how to be cruel, punished the Athenians by making their daughters mad and driving them to suicide. Tragic drinking which brings about death upon death.

Wine is a blessing only if one masters its strength. Thought of by the Greeks as a *pharmakon* − a poison and a remedy at the same time, depending upon how one uses it − it is a drug which must be socially controlled, and this is where the Greek manners of proper drinking apply. In principle, wine is never consumed pure; it should be diluted with water, mixed in varying proportions which will determine the strength of the drink. Particular vessels are used for this purpose: amphoras carry the wine and hydrias the water, and they are mixed in a krater (from the verb *kerannumi,* to mix); a vase called an oinochoe is used to draw and pour for the guests into the cups for drinking *(kylix* or *skyphos)*. The skill of the potters would come later still, pushing the sophistication to the point of throwing double-walled vases or coolers *(psykter)* to keep the drink at an agreeable temperature.

Such a diversity of forms gave the painters an extremely varied choice of surfaces to decorate: circular medallions on the insides of cups, large friezes on the kraters, panels on the amphoras, with or without a marked frame; many solutions existed and allowed the exploration of a single theme according to the different formats.

In decorating their drinking vases, painters often chose motifs related to drinking and the *symposion,* that moment of conviviality where everyone drinks together, where one divides up and distributes the wine of Dionysos to all.

But before it can take place, one must get oneself to the *symposion,* go to the houses of friends bringing a drinking vase and singing of it with music. A plate signed by the painter Epictetos perfectly captures the

moment. A bearded, slightly paunchy adult is headed to the party, crowned with ivy. He wears boots and carries on his shoulder a long stick over which he has hung his cloak. In his right hand he holds a large *skyphos* which he brandishes in front of him. His head is raised, his mouth open; is he singing, perhaps? On his left side at his thigh hangs a sort of speckled holster which finishes in a fringed double point: this is a holster for the *aulos,* a double flute made of reed, the customary instrument at banquets. One can see this instrument and its holster better on another plate, a match for the first, also signed by Epictetos. It is not a human drinker but a more agitated satyr who figures here, turning around, the two *aulos* pipes in his hands. His penis is erect, as is often the case with satyrs, and it serves him well for hanging the holster glimpsed on the other plate. The difference in manners between humans and satyrs is characteristic of the Dionysian universe of the satyrs, to which we shall return. But let us note here that to the visual parody is added a game of words to which Aristophanes gives us the key: the *aulos* holster is called a *subene,* which is evocative of the erotic expression *su binein,* "fuck you." Wine, song, music and erotic jokes; these are truly the ingredients for a procession of merrymakers and drinkers.

This festive promenade, before or after drinking, is called *comos,* a cortege. The Greek term refers to all types of occasions and processions, but archaeologists have developed the habit of applying it almost mechanically to images of this type, which feature a drinker en route, taking part in the *comos.* In seeing him pass, it is as if the viewer is invited to follow him and to enter into the dance.

Most of the images of *comos* show a group in movement, carried along by the music of the *aulos.* A fragment of a cup attributed to Onesimos depicts a young woman with her cheeks puffed out blowing into a double *aulos* held by the nimble fingers of her two hands. The fine transparent garment allows the viewer to make out her peaked breasts and her angled thigh, carried away in dance. On her left arm hangs her cloak. The rest of the medallion is lost, but a hand on her shoulder shows she was accompanied by another individual, probably a drinking companion who leans on her and dances or staggers along to the concert. Although it is a fragment, this cup reveals the close connection which exists between music, dance, eroticism and the march to the *symposion.*

The collective character of the *symposion* is often explicit on very large vases. Although the medallion isolates one figure, the surface of the kraters or the exterior of the cups allows for the ample unfolding of the representation of the drinkers among them. The Kleophrades painter joined six drinkers on a *psykter,* which is today in Princeton. All are stretched out on a sort of long mattress, their chests turned to the right, leaning on cushions, singing, drinking and playing. They wear crowns of leaves. One of them, with a beard, prepares to drink from one cup while lifting another in his right hand. At his side, a young beardless man holds a *skyphos* in one hand and in the other a cup whose top-shaped foot prohibits placing it down before having emptied it. The gesture of his right hand is remarkable: he holds the cup by the handle with the tips of his fingers. He is playing a game

16. ATTIC RED-FIGURE CUP, FRAGMENT, ONESIMOS
490 BC, PRESERVED HEIGHT 0.11 M
PARIS, CABINET DES MÉDAILLES, BIBLIOTHÈQUE NATIONALE

called *kottabos*, which consists of launching with the cup a few drops of wine at a target. In doing this, one dedicates the shot to a partner; if the throw is successful, it is a sign of amorous success. Wine and the erotic are thus joined together in a concrete way, in a game which puts to the test the skill and mastery of drinkers who are more or less intoxicated. Further on, another guest sings, with lyre in hand and head thrown back, supported by his right hand.

Below this uninterrupted scene runs an ornamental frieze where different vases and accessories of the banquet stand out in silhouette: some baskets, two little dogs, and a stick; among the vases there is one in the form of a *phallos,* as if the potter anticipated the desires of the drinkers.

The unbroken pictorial surface on this *psykter* takes practically the form of a cylinder, which thus recreates the actual space of the banquet room. The drinkers are in fact never very numerous; a room generally consists of seven to twelve beds arranged end to end against the walls, so that nothing happens behind the back of the guests. They are all reclining face to face, each within sight and sound of all the others. Even if the room is architecturally square or rectangular, the metaphor of the circle perfectly suits the group of drinkers, with complete equality among them.

17. ATTIC RED-FIGURE PSYKTER, KLEOPHRADES PAINTER
500 BC, HEIGHT 0.34 M
PRINCETON ART MUSEUM

On a cup attributed to Douris, one finds again an analogous structure with different graphic solutions and new iconographic details. The motif of the *symposion* is found on the inside as well as the outside of the cup. On the medallion appears a solitary drinker on an elevated bed, a *kline,* before whom is placed a table from which hang wreaths of foliage. He holds out his cup at the end of his arm, returning it as if to ask for a drink. Along his arm one reads the word *kalos,* "beautiful." On the other side, one finds three beds, two seen in length and the third on the right seen on its narrow end, so that the drinker who lies there appears from behind. The viewer of the image, himself on a banquet bed, is led by this foreshortening – infrequent in Attic imagery – to consider himself as forming the third side of the banquet room. The pictorial surface which is here in the form of a disk proposes then another metaphorical equivalence for representing the circularity of the banquet space. Moreover, in retaining here the effect of foreshortening which works upon the space of the viewer, Douris adds an extra dimension to the plastic investigations of his predecessors. The drinker who uses this cup is in effect implicated in a reflexive image, so to speak, in which the drinkers are shown holding the same type of cup as the one on which they are depicted.

On the main surface in the center of the image, an *aulos* player stands. To the left, another nude adolescent, a *pais,* is serving the banqueters. He holds in one hand a small round jug and in the other a sort of sieve, no doubt made of bronze, which serves to filter the impurities of the wine. The guest lying in the center caresses his beard and seems absorbed in thought and in listening to the *aulos* player. The other two raise their cups at arms length; the one on the right turns it on its handle and plays *kottabos*. Behind the musician upon a tall support of bronze rests a lamp, which indicates the nocturnal character of the meeting and perhaps serves as a target for the wine throwers.

The drinker on the left side has an interesting hairstyle which reminds us of the Phrygian cap used as a symbol of liberty during the French revolution. It is actually a Scythian cap, or at least the hairstyle Attic painters gave to Scythian archers. Yet our drinker has nothing about him of the barbarian, nothing which distinguishes him otherwise from his companions. Such a hairstyle sets him apart as the symposiarch, the master of the banquet, who will determine the rules of the game in the course of the evening. As previously indicated, the proportions of the mixture of water and wine could vary, and consequently, the strength of the wine that is served. It is the symposiarch who decides this, if agreement is not made on its own. He also decides the number of kraters to be served and the themes to be taken up for singing and discussing among friends. He is in a way the regulating authority for this temporary society; his existence does not impose itself, but it is sometimes mentioned in the texts, and indicated here by this "Scythian" mark. It should be added here that the Scythians were for the Greeks what the Poles were in the 19th century to the French, who, in saying *"saoul comme un Polonais"* ("drunk as a Pole") meant to indicate an unacceptable limit. What is said of Others teaches us not about the others but about the one who says it. For the Greeks, to drink like a Scythian – *skuthizien* – is to drink pure wine and therefore risk total drunkenness and the uncontrollable folly which is inflicted by Dionysos upon those who do not know how to master the wine. On the Douris cup, the master of ceremonies indicated by the Scythian mark maintains his control and assures the *symposion* of dignity and good behavior.

18, 19. ATTIC RED-FIGURE CUP, DOURIS
490 BC, HEIGHT 0.28 M
FLORENCE, ARCHAEOLOGICAL MUSEUM

20, 21. ATTIC RED-FIGURE CUP, DOURIS
490 BC, HEIGHT 0.28 M
FLORENCE, ARCHAEOLOGICAL MUSEUM

In the background of the image are found vases which come in order one after the other: cups and jugs for pouring, drinking, and serving, in turn and nearly endlessly. The vases are here again a pictogram of the *symposion*.

The *aulos* is not the only musical instrument of the *symposion*. It has as a complement the lyre, or an oblong version thereof with lower-pitched strings, the *barbiton*. Lyre and *aulos* are often in competition, at least in the mythical story which sets Apollo and Marsyas against each other. The latter, a very accomplished satyr, received the *aulos* from Athena, who had just invented it to imitate the cries of the Gorgons lamenting their sister Medusa, who was decapitated by Perseus. The goddess was the first to play this instrument, but when she saw herself, with cheeks puffed out and deformed, she rejected it, and it was Marsyas who had the misfortune of picking it up. A true satyr, he didn't worry about ugliness; a virtuoso musician, he bragged of playing the *aulos* better than Apollo played the lyre. In his pride he defied the god. The Phrygian king Midas was chosen as the judge; he

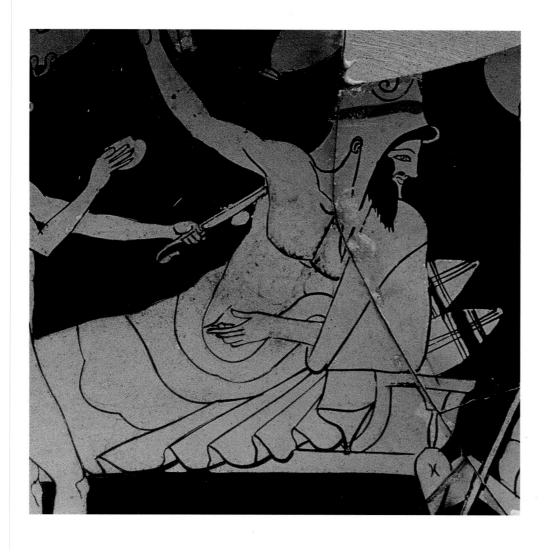

declared Marsyas the winner. But Apollo would not accept this; he gave Midas the ears of an ass and in turn challenged Marsyas to play his instrument upside down or to sing while playing, both of which are impossible with the *aulos*. The satyr was defeated; his pride was fatal. Apollo, the sacrificer, with knife in hand, avenged himself cruelly. Marsyas is flayed alive, dismembered by the vengeful god.

Not all is harmonious on Olympus, and music does not necessarily seem to make manners milder, at least in these mythical times. At the *symposion,* lyre and *aulos* make a better couple, even though Alcibiades in Plato's *Symposium* reminds us of his aversion for the *aulos* which disfigures and his preference for the more noble lyre since it leaves the voice free.

On the neck of an amphora attributed to Euphronios, one sees a lyre player at the banquet, stretched out on the ground, his back propped up with a cushion, according to the usual sketch. His fingers placed upon the strings, he holds up his lyre, the frame of which is made of

turtle shell. Crowned, head raised, he sings and the painter has taken care to inscribe his song near his mouth. The letters are not separated from the image – as for example the bubbles in a comic strip. They are part of it and stretch out in a circular arc around the head of the singer, who is therefore haloed with music. The text is not in perfect Greek, but one can read – and hear – *mameokapoteo,* which comes close to the beginning of a poem by Sappho: *maomai kai poteo,* "I suffer and I desire." A song of love, characteristic of the poetry of the banquet, the poem is completed on the opposite side by the image of a *kottabos* player who tries his luck at a game of love.

The poetry made to be recited at the banquet holds an essential place in the archaic lyric and one can consider that the major part of the poems we know, those from Anacreon to Pindar, and from Sappho to Alcaeus, were recited at the *symposion.* Among drinkers, the poetic memory fully plays its role; each one sings and recites in his turn passages which make up the common culture of the archaic world.

The repertoire is not limited to erotic poetry. Epic and heroic themes have an important place there, as do hymns in honor of the gods. As testimony of that are two unconnected fragments of a cup by the Brygos painter. On the first, a young, beardless man, with a crown, turns to his neighbor on the right, of whom we see only an arm holding out a cup in order to be served; in the background a sword is suspended above them. The presence of arms, rare at a *symposion* during this time period, seems to suggest here a military or heroic sociability. On the second fragment, near the shoulder of the first drinker, who is on the left, hangs a display of weapons: a large round shield whose circle is interrupted by the lip of the vase, decorated with a bird in silhouette, and a pair of greaves – cnemides –, shin protectors made of bronze standing in front of the shield. To the right a drinker sings, with his head thrown back and held in his upraised arms; his mouth is open, allowing letters which are read from right to left to escape according to a dynamic trajectory which makes visible the uttered song: *opolon,* "O, Apollo." This is the beginning of a hymn in honor of the god who is a musician and singer *par excellence.* As one sees, the song unfurls in the image which thus takes on a sonorous dimension which is essential to the *symposion.* As much as does the wine, the music and the poetry circulate among the drinkers, and the painters of the cups try to give an account of that.

24, 25. ATTIC RED-FIGURE CUP, FRAGMENTS, BRYGOS PAINTER
480 BC, PRESERVED SIZE 0.09 BY 0.10 M
PARIS, CABINET DES MÉDAILLES, BIBLIOTHÈQUE NATIONALE

The Greek manners of drinking, founded first and foremost upon mixing and sharing, make conviviality the key to the *symposion*. From this point of view, the vases, which are technical objects necessary for the practice of good drinking, acquire a very strong symbolic value. The krater is not only the vase which allows the mixing; in the pictorial process it is the focal point around which the space of the banquet is organized and can by itself signify metonymically the set of values it has come to evoke.

It is in this way that one can understand the medallion of a cup in the Louvre, on which there appears by itself on the inside of the vase a krater crowned with ivy. The vase is treated like a guest, adorned as they are in Dionysian greenery. Before the krater stands a young naked man with a crown, a *pais* come to draw drink and serve the guests. The jug in one hand, a cup in the other, he circulates the wine and uses in a dynamic way the same vases that we have seen hanging in the background on the Douris cup, like pictograms of the banquet. On the outside of this same cup one finds the complete scene: six drinkers in a circle. But on the medallion, the krater and the other vases function in the hands of the young man like a table service, which is enough to evoke the pleasure of drinking together and sharing among friends, to the sound of *aulos* and lyre.

These manners of drinking which characterize Greek culture are reaffirmed in mythology in the many stories which call them into question. Each of these stories puts us in a time or place which is unaware of the good use of wine.

One story treats the adventures of Herakles with the centaurs. On a small black-figure lekythos, the hero, clad in a lion skin, has opened a large half-buried jar – a *pithos* – the cover of which he holds raised. In his other hand, he draws the wine with an oinochoe under the watch of a centaur who holds out his hand towards the hero's jug. In the background are hanging Herakles' bow and quiver, as well as his clothes. The scene is framed by a woman at the left, whose presence is unexpected, and a young man at the right, the young Iolaos, the companion of Herakles on his exploits. The jar at the center of the image is a gift Dionysos made to the centaurs, telling them not to touch it until the arrival of Herakles among them. Therefore, they can only open and share it with him, according to Greek laws of hospitality. The centaur in front of Herakles is Pholos; he is a good

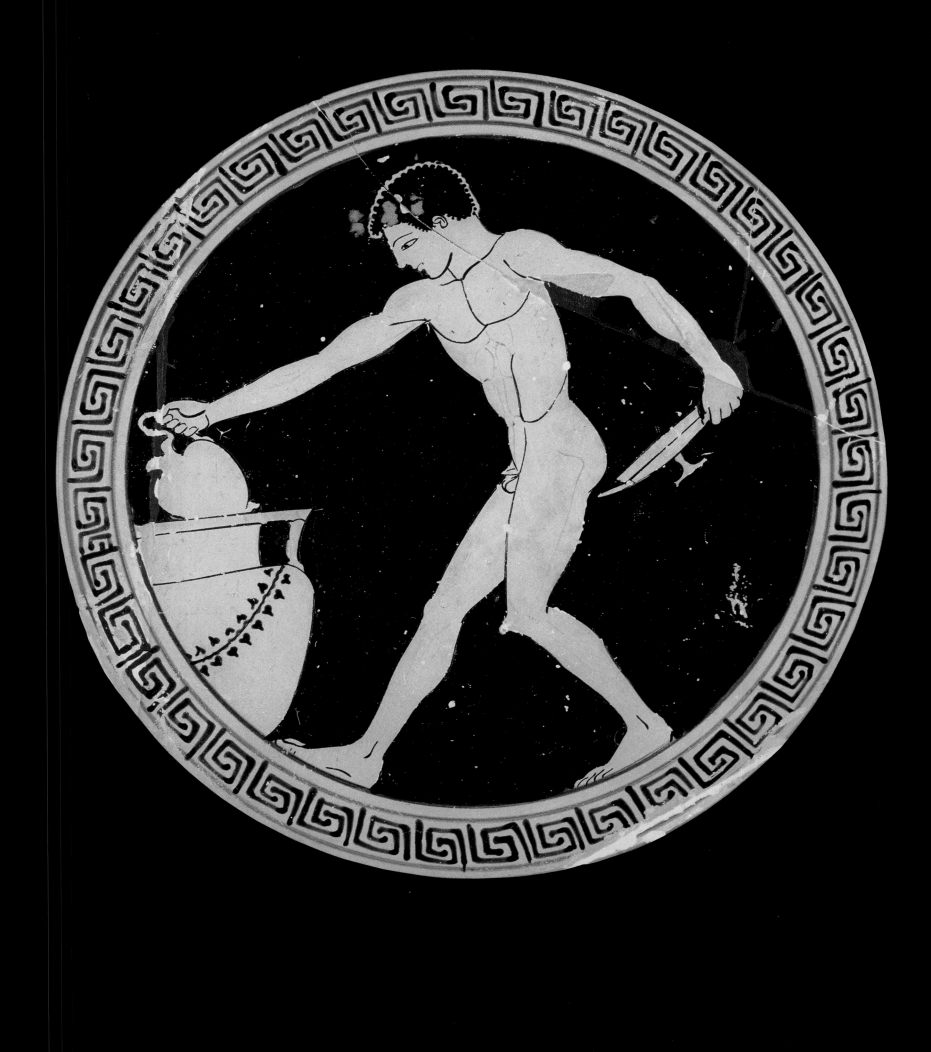

27. ATTIC BLACK-FIGURE LEKYTHOS DRAWING, PHOLOS PAINTER
490-480 BC. HEIGHT 0.27 M
PARIS, CABINET DES MÉDAILLES, BIBLIOTHÈQUE NATIONALE
▶ **28, 29.** TWO VIEWS OF THE VASE, FIGURE 27.

centaur, one who welcomes the hero appropriately. But as soon as the jar is opened, the very scent of the pure wine is enough to attract his less civilized fellow creatures. They rush up and attack Herakles who must resist and battle them; the scene of hospitality degenerates into a pitched battle. On the small lekythos the painter has remembered the moment of the opening of the jar; everything is still going well between Herakles and Pholos. But the story does not stay this way, and it is to face the imminent danger of the centaurs that Iolaos turns to the right. In the savage world of the centaurs, between their human nature and their animal nature, the manners of Greek drinking and sociability do not find a place.

The same happens in the land of the Cyclopes, but in a different way. These one-eyed monsters do not live in a community; they have no city, no city walls, and they do not acknowledge the gods. Isolated, each for himself, they raise their herds without knowledge of agriculture, or, *a fortiori,* of wine. When Odysseus is returning from Troy, tossed on the sea by the will of Poseidon who pursues him in enmity, it is among them that he runs aground. He and his companions are captured by one of them, Polyphemus, who imprisons them all in his cave and, delighted by this arrival of fresh flesh, intends to eat them one by one, moving from a quasi-vegetarian diet to a scandalously cannibal one. One knows the double trick, the *metis,* of Odysseus. To the Cyclops who asks who he is, Odysseus responds "My name is Nobody *(outis),*"[1] and then asks him to taste the wine he carries with him in a wineskin. The Cyclops has no knowledge of this

1. Homer, *Odyssey,* Book IX, 355-70 ; Euripides, *Cyclops,* 548-49.

beverage and begins to drink it pure, by himself. Thrilled by this discovery, by way of thanks, he promises to eat Odysseus last. In the version of Euripides, which embellishes that of Homer, the Cyclops wants to make a profit off his companions with this discovery. But Odysseus dissuades him – the arrival of other Cyclopes would be fatal for him – and recommends that he keep it all for himself and not share any of it. Thus the Cyclops is unaware of mixing and doesn't dream of sharing. Once drunk, he falls asleep. Odysseus, helped by his companions, blinds the Cyclops by gouging out his one eye with a large stake strengthened in fire.

◄ 30. BLACK-FIGURE LAKONIAN CUP, RIDER PAINTER
560 BC. MAXIMUM DIAMETER 0.29 M
PARIS, CABINET DES MÉDAILLES, BIBLIOTHÈQUE NATIONALE

This is what is shown on a Lakonian cup from around 560 BC, which takes up in a synthetic manner the story we know from the *Odyssey*. The Cyclops is seated at the right upon a rock and holds in his hands the legs of one of Odysseus' companions, three-quarters eaten. Before the Cyclops a young man, perhaps Odysseus himself, holds out a kantharos full of the fatal wine. Four solid strapping fellows then come forward, the stake on their shoulders piercing the eye of the Cyclops. Above, a serpent indicates the space of the cave where Odysseus and his men are imprisoned. The image accumulates the elements belonging to the successive moments of the story: the cannibalism of the monster, the wine which intoxicates him, the stake which blinds him. It doesn't tell the tale just as we have done, but it shows the driving elements of the story. It is up to the drinker, in taking up his cup, to engage with this image and to conjure up if he wishes the well-known narrative.

He can also remind his guests what are the manners of the table, the good use of wine, and how, in the savage world where Odysseus was led astray, ignorance of the powers of wine can transform the most ferocious monster into a dozing drunk and how all together the companions of Odysseus came up against an apparently colossal force, much like Dionysos, who, in serving wine, knew how to bend the will of Hephaistos, master of the Cyclopes of Etna, cousins of Polyphemus, in order to bring him back to Olympus.

UNDER THE GAZE OF EROS 2

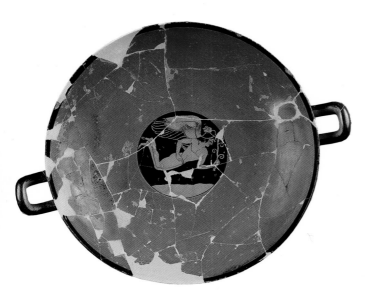

Eros rules the world. Or at least he is the driving force behind it, if one believes Hesiod and his *Theogony*. The divine powers can only emerge from the primordial chaos after his intervention, which allows, by the internal division of a world that was formerly closed, the engendering of the gods. Eros is therefore a power of beginnings, a force which sets the world in motion. This figure of archaic cosmogonies, for whom there exists no image, is very different from the Eros sung by the poets and celebrated at the symposium on drinking vases.

The Eros of the banquet takes on the appearance of a beautiful adolescent with powerful wings, often similar in his attitudes and gestures to humans, of whom he is like an emanation. Different from the Roman Cupids, plump babies who reappear as the round cherubs of the Renaissance, the Attic Greek Eros has the look of a handsome young man whose elegance the painters so often acclaim.

A cup from around the year 510 BC furnishes us with a remarkable example. A young man with large shoulders turned towards us, but with the rest of his body in profile, flies horizontally, his wings spread above an area whose undulating surface indicates that it is the sea. This isolated Eros, outside of any context, crossing over the maritime space, has the aspect of a symbolic figure. He holds in his left hand a branch embellished with curls and a floral bud. This plant-like element is closer to the ornaments which painters place on the border of an image, under the handles for example, or on the necks of large vases, than to a real flower such as we sometimes see in the hands of women or of gods. The deliberate variation between the rendering of the winged figure and that of the plant-like branch, more stylized but nonetheless integrated within the depiction, indicates the symbolic value of these flowers, which are not just extra material, but the very place where beauty – and desire – settle themselves. Eros is a living ornament and the ornaments which he carries with him are both beautiful and desirable.

The painter emphasized the importance of this figure on the medallion of the cup, by using a particular technique of glazing called "red coral" to cover the interior surface of the vase. By the working of oxidation and reduction during the firing of the vase, the glazes blacken or else fade into a deep red more vivid than that of terracotta, closer to the color of coral. What is sometimes produced by accident, during an over-firing, is here perfectly mastered and permits obtaining an unusual colorful intensity which highlights the figure of Eros.

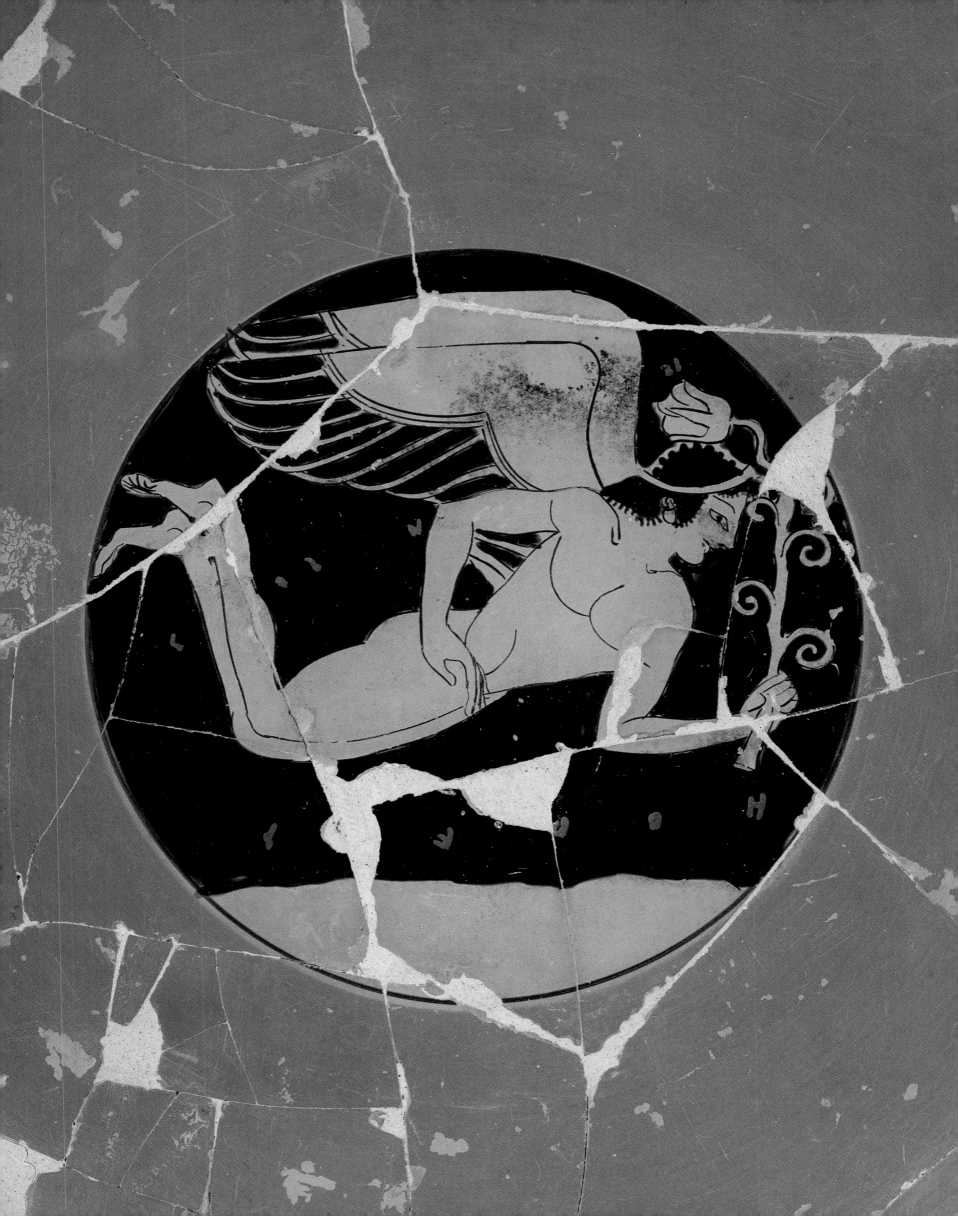

Finally the painter has placed along the length of the body of beautiful Eros an inscription which is read at first from left to right, from the elbow to the ankle, *kalos,* "beautiful," then in turning the cup, along the line of the waves, *ho pais,* "young man." The formula is banal; we have already encountered it and it will come up again. This leitmotif, *ho pais kalos,* "the handsome young man," is not perceptible here except by manipulating the cup, by turning it in your hands or by turning the view – the eye? – around Eros. The young man we are looking at in this way could well be Eros himself, or any other young man, left anonymous by the painter. It is up to the drinker to choose and to specify if necessary, according to the context, this generic evocation so frequent on drinking vases.

The winged god flies before our eyes, just above the sea of wine which fills the bottom of the cup, admirably inscribed by a series of graphic and plastic procedures which emphasize his beauty: his isolation, the ornament which he carries, the brilliant red which surrounds him, and finally the inscription whose letters stand out like stars on the visual field.

If the Greek eroticism which displays itself at the symposium seems to prefer above any other figure that of the handsome young man, it does not limit itself to an exclusive masculine homosexuality. After generations of Hellenists pretended for a long time to ignore or greatly minimize this homosexuality, which seemed to contradict the model of a miraculous Greece which brought laws to our Christian West, many scholars have studied the nature of the relationships between adults and adolescents, the simultaneously erotic and pedagogic bond which it implies, and the passive and transitory character of the status of the *eromenos,* of the young man who is loved and modeled by his lover, the *erastes.*

What will hold us here is the importance of this erotic relationship in the world of the symposium and the work of aestheticization which it implies on the part of the vase painters. They often sought to show not only the presence of Eros at the banquet or at the palaestra, and the pleasure which this presence implies, but also the gaze focused upon the love object – be it a perfect young man or woman – by the adult spectators.

A cup signed by the potter Hieron plays in a very clear way upon these different registers, masculine and feminine, erotic and didactic. On the medallion, a young man with an athletic build, staff wedged under his arm, leans towards a young girl who holds little flowers at the tips of her fingers. It is not the large wings of Eros in flight, but more discreet flowers which simultaneously evoke color and perfume.

The exterior of the vase is entirely occupied by scenes which tell about adults and *paides*. On one surface two adolescents are seated, one playing a double *aulos,* the other holding a lyre, the two instruments which occupy an essential place at the symposium. In a chiasmus, so that each man has near him something that belongs to the other, next to the lyre player is suspended an *aulos* holster and next to the *aulos* player is a lyre: a subtle counterpoint which highlights the complementarity of these instruments in Greek music education. These two young men are framed by three standing adults who are bearded and crowned; leaning on their staffs, they seem to listen admiringly to the sound of the *aulos.* It is music in images, but also spectacle: the young men are beautiful to see for those who listen to them, and the gaze focused upon them on the inside of the image is intensified by that of the drinkers, who, in turn, cup in hand, gaze upon the show.

On the other side, one finds again the same bearded adults, still leaning on their staffs, stopped in front of three partners. In the middle, the young man reveals himself by holding a hare by the ears and back legs; a living gift which he has just received, the hare is part of the lovers' gifts, simultaneously game and a metaphor for the erotic hunt which brings *erastes* (lover) and *eromenos* (loved one) face to face. Behind him, in the background of the image, is suspended a pack —

33. ATTIC RED-FIGURE CUP, MACRON
SIGNED BY THE POTTER HIERON
490 BC, DIAMETER 0.33 M
VIENNA KUNSTHISTORISCHES MUSEUM

▶▶ 34. DETAIL OF VASE, FIGURE 33.

strigil, sponge and net sack – the mark of the athletic practice which builds attractive bodies. The two other young men are very modestly wrapped in their cloaks, which allow only the head to be seen. Immobile, they are not yet allowed to seduce, even though the adult at the left lifts before the face of the young man a purse with supposedly tempting contents: anklebones to play with, or actual money? Archaeologists disagree, but the theory that it is a game, played with anklebones, or *astragaloi,* and therefore less mercenary, would of course seem more attractive.

The range of erotic gifts is not infinite. If the contents of the purses could seem problematic, the other gifts are more easily identifiable; aside from the flowers already mentioned, the most frequent gifts are animals, birds or small game. In the iconography of the game of seduction, the painters at the beginning of the 5th century BC preferred the games of approach, such as the ones we have just seen – contemplation, conversation, the exchange of gifts – while their predecessors, at the end of the 6th century BC, in black-figure painting, preferred scenes where the adults possess their partners in a more explicit way. But the Amasis painter, from 540 BC, on a cup which is today in the Louvre, has generously displayed the game of approach and of seduction, in aligning a series of partners and gifts, alternating heterosexual and homosexual couples. Each of the two sides is composed according to the same scheme, with three couples face to face. On the first, in the center, brilliantly white in her nudity, a woman stands completely unclothed – which is exceptional outside of bathing scenes – adorned only with a necklace and earrings, a flower and a crown in her hands. Before her stands a bearded adult who offers a chicken. To the right is a homosexual couple: a young man holds a small round vase, an aryballos, whose perfumed oils serve to coat the bodies of athletes, as well as a lance, which makes him a hunter. Facing him, a bearded adult offers a swan. To the left, the young man holds a lance; his partner carries a doe, more substantial game, which refers back to the hunting exercises.

The other side is constructed in the same way, with man and woman in the center; but here there is no gift: only the game of gestures marks the beginning of a dialogue. To the left, an adult offers a cock to a young man; to the right a dead hare is presented to a young hunter. Finally, under each handle is found an isolated adult. One, seated on a chair, holds a chicken; the other, squatting, holds a panther *(pardalis).*

Since the chicken fits easily into the series of small animals which are offered as gifts, the presence of a panther is surprising. But the animal, in the Greek imagination, is associated with perfume and seduction; the wearing of a panther skin characterized not only the maenads, companions of Dionysos, as we shall see, but also certain dancers and guests at the banquet.

In thus alternating masculine and feminine, the Amasis painter indicates the Greek bisexuality which brings together, without exclusivity, homo- and heterosexual relationships, in a culture which, though highly masculine, was not ignorant of feminine charms.

The image of women in the Attic ceramic repertoire is as complex and varied as the relations between men and women. In them one also sees certain aspects in their ritual or mythic contexts; as well as the role of the wife, in relation to the warrior and in the domestic sphere. Grooming, perfume and finery are also part of the repertoire, as well as the image of women's work, which appears beautiful to see and good to show.

The representation of desire and of seduction is not exclusively limited to vases for the banquet. An oblong perfume vase, an alabastron, represents such an encounter between a man and a woman. Seated, she plays with a small doe while holding a flower. Behind her is a flared basket, the *calathos,* which contains the wool which women work, and in the background is a small lekythos – another type of perfume vase – as well as a circular disk mirror. He stands upright, leaning on his staff; his cloak has slipped and allows a view of his naked torso. He holds in his right hand an oblong vase, hanging at the end of a long strap, which echoes, in image, the vase upon which it appears. The man thus offers perfume to the woman, who is seen here in the space which is most often her own: in the house, attending to both domestic work and her self-adornment. But the work suggested by the basket of wool has nothing to do with tiresome labor; moreover, nothing which suggests difficulty or fatigue is shown here. The iconographic genre seeks not to represent the reality of domestic life, which Xenophon would call the economic, the art of managing the *oikos,* of directing a household and its slaves, but rather to accentuate feminine beauty and its spectacular character: this is clearly not a sociological document on daily life in Greece. This type of visit, often represented on drinking vases as well as on those for perfume, is meant

37. FULL VIEW OF ATTIC BLACK-FIGURE ALABASTRON
EMPORION PAINTER, 500 BC, HEIGHT 0.15 M
PARIS, CABINET DES MÉDAILLES, BIBLIOTHÈQUE NATIONALE
▶ 38, 39. TWO VIEWS OF THE VASE, FIGURE

to be seen both by women at their dressing table and by men at the banquet. For the latter, the vase offers the seductive representation of women as they are pleased to imagine them; for the former, it puts forward a model of modest elegance which they are invited to follow. The genre of "the woman at her toilette" is therefore almost always susceptible to a double reading, masculine and feminine.

The painters have multiplied the variations and groupings of images around these motifs – grooming, work, and gifts – thus creating a whole series of echoes between masculine and feminine. Two examples appear on cups in the Archaeological Museum in Florence.

The first involves a *comast,* on the medallion, as we have seen in the preceding chapter: he advances with cup in hand. The two very similar sides of the cup present subtle variations. In both cases, a woman stands in the center of the image, framed by two young men leaning on their staffs, in the posture of an onlooker in a conversation. On each of the two sides, the character on the left holds a flower at the tips of his fingers, a sign of beauty and seduction. On one of the sides, the woman, with arms outstretched, holds in one hand a flower and in the other hand a staff for holding wool. The symmetry which her bearing creates between these two objects highlights the equivalence between weaving wool and feminine beauty. The opposite side confirms this reading: the woman at the center of the image, under the gaze of the two men who frame her, carries a *calathos,* the emblematic object of her activity in the

oikos. Hence, this cup combines on the interior the purely masculine world of the symposium and on the exterior the flowery meeting of men and women around the weaving of wool.

The other cup proposes a similar combination, but one which is decidedly more clear-cut. On the medallion appears a young cavalier. He wears an embroidered cloak and the standard cap, and high boots with flaps in the Thracian style which characterizes Athenian horsemen of this period, approximately 470 BC (cf. fig. 70). From the hindquarters to the head of the horse, one reads the familiar inscription: *ho pais kalos*. The image sends us back not to the symposium and the vase itself, as before, but to military activity. The world of men is here that of horsemen, of Athenian high society, seen not from the side of combats and bloody trials, but in its most seductive light, as in a parade where the young men are beautiful to see.

On the exterior there figure only women among themselves. On one side they hold in succession a crown, a branch with fruit, another crown, a branch and an alabastron; in the background one finds again crowns and sandals, and under the handles are a stool and a *calathos*.

43. INTERIOR OF ATTIC RED-FIGURE CUP, PISTOXENOS PAINTER
470 BC, DIAMETER 0.32 M
FLORENCE, ARCHAEOLOGICAL MUSEUM

On the other side, the two seated women make the crowns; the one upright to the left stands near a *calathos,* the one on the right is in the process of spinning wool, distaff in hand. Very close to her, in the background, hangs a mirror. One will notice the formal analogy between these two objects, distaff and mirror, often so close that it is difficult to separate and to identify the objects with any certainty. The ambiguity seems intentional and confirms the connection already noted between grooming and women's work.

On this cup the two worlds, masculine and feminine, do not interfere with one another: they are placed in parallel. From the horseman in movement: the exterior space to the interior of the vase; from the seated women: the interior of the *oikos* to the exterior of the cup. But in both cases, circling around the entire image, the formula inscribes *ho pais kalos*. Although the image seems to divide masculine and feminine equally, the inscriptions refer only to the masculine world, that of those who use the cups.

While the cups, by the play of internal and external surfaces, allow subtle combinations of complementary and opposite images, the same does not apply to all types of vases. Lekythoi containing perfumed oil present – like the alabastrons – a reduced cylindrical surface and often allow only for an isolated figure. This is the case in the production of certain workshops who specialized in this form, and of painters who worked in a standardized way, not with figures which are mechanically repetitive, but with variations in reduced numbers from the same scheme.

One can observe that an anonymous painter from the 430's BC (called the Klügmann painter) decorated about forty lekythoi, among which only two represent a male character. All the others feature women, always isolated, from different points of view. Only their clothes or the objects they hold produce a specific context which allows us to situate them. A large number of these lekythoi derive from the previously described models: one sees on them a woman with a box, a basket of wool or an alabastron, which returns us to the domestic sphere and to work seen not as labor but as seductive activity. Others show a woman with a musical instrument – lyre, tambourine, or even a harp – intended to charm the listener as well as the spectator.

This painter also produced divine or mythic figures: with a palm tree and a bow, he obtains Artemis; with arms, a shield or a trumpet, an Amazon, the mythic model of the inconceivable woman warrior. In both cases these choices follow a logic which returns us to a universe without men: the Amazons, as is known, refuse to marry and they murder their male children. As for Artemis, she is a fierce virgin, a huntress who accompanies young girls to the threshold of marriage, before giving them up to Aphrodite and Hera.

Obviously, it would be naïve to believe that the Klügmann painter is a woman – even though that would not be unthinkable – but his taste for the variations on the feminine model is remarkable. A lekythos in the Louvre is at the crossroads of two series, mythic and domestic. One sees on it a woman standing before an open box from which she has taken a scroll which she opens before her. In isolating such an object, which implies some literary knowledge and a competence in reading linked with poetic recitation, he makes this woman into a Muse, either literally or more likely metaphorically. It is no longer work which beautifies the woman and makes her desirable, but her poetic and musical knowledge, placed on the open field of a perfume vase.

By means of this laboratory of the feminine which is constituted by the series of lekythoi attributed to the Klügmann painter, one sees very well the extent to which the Attic image functions as an open system of

45 TO 48. SERIES OF ATTIC RED-FIGURE LEKYTHOI
KLÜGMANN PAINTER, 430 BC
WÜRZBURG UNIVERSITY, HEIGHT 0.27 M;
LAON, ARCHAEOLOGICAL MUSEUM, HEIGHT 0.27 M;
HEIDELBERG UNIVERSITY, PRESERVED HEIGHT 0.16 M;
MILAN, ARCHAEOLOGICAL MUSEUM, PRESERVED HEIGHT 0.22 M

▶ 49. ATTIC RED-FIGURE LEKYTHOS, KLÜGMANN PAINTER
430 BC, HEIGHT 0.25 M
PARIS, LOUVRE

symbols which changes its forms from the divine to the human, from the imaginary war to the domestic space, without ever fixing itself upon a particular story or episode. These images tell nothing in particular; they present for us each time an aspect of the feminine: venerable like Artemis, frightening like the Amazons, or seductive like the workers and the musicians.

At the same time, around 420 BC, when Athens was erecting the Parthenon, the figure of Eros experienced some transformations in relation to the model of a handsome young man such as we have seen at the end of the archaic period. His size decreased though he remained an adolescent; his reduced scale in relation to the other figures in the image makes him an actor who circulates in the space of the representation, a bit like the palm leaves and ornaments.

On a *skyphos* in the Louvre, two women are represented, one on each side. On one side the woman stands upright, coffer and mirror in hand, according to the usual scheme. On the other she sits with Eros on her knees. It has often been suggested that what we have here is Aphrodite playing with her son, since her familiarity with Eros gives her a maternal air. But it seems that the painter wanted to show not a goddess and her offspring but rather the divine presence of Eros in the feminine sphere. Desire shows itself at the side of the women who are gazed upon by the viewer; in integrating Eros into the image, the painter presents for us that which creates the beauty of women when they are grooming and gazing upon themselves in the mirror.

One can find the counter-proof of this analysis by comparing this image to certain bronze mirrors from the 5th century BC. On one of them, the reflective surface is surrounded with remarkable ornaments: a woman holding a dove serves as the stand; at her shoulders fly two figures of Eros who are both companions to her as well as the emanation of the image which has just been reflected on the surface of polished bronze. When she looks at herself in the mirror, the woman sees herself surrounded by this flight of Cupids, companions of Aphrodite and a sign of her allure. At the top of the mirror stands a Sphinx, guardian of the feminine secret, while around the metal disk two dogs chase two hares, reminding us that the hunt is a constant metaphor for amorous pursuit, and that the hare, as we have seen, is one of the erotic gifts.

And so, under the gaze of Eros, the woman who is grooming herself becomes a favored object of the masculine gaze.

◀ **50.** ATTIC RED-FIGURE SKYPHOS, SHUVALOV PAINTER
420 BC, HEIGHT 0.09 M
PARIS, LOUVRE

51. BRONZE MIRROR, PELOPONNESIAN (?)
460-50 BC, HEIGHT 0.41 M
NEW YORK, METROPOLITAN MUSEUM OF ART

ATHLETES, GAMES, COMPETITIONS   3

The modern notion of sport did not exist in ancient Greece. The words designating the sort of activities which we would call sports refer to the competition, to the battle and the prize which one wins as a result. It is, after all, the rivalry and the spirit of competition which characterize this world in which one does not seek to achieve a specific result – there is always something to be improved – but where one measures oneself against others at a given moment in a specific place. One does not beat a record, one beats a competitor. Of these ephemeral events, which are linked to festivals in honor of the gods, nothing is recorded apart from the names of the victors.

The Greek word *athlon* in the singular designates the prize which one carries off at the time of the competition, and in the plural – *athla* – the events, the games where the athletes meet. One can read this term – inscribed like a legend alongside the signature of the painter Sophilos – on a fragmentary vase representing the funeral games in honor of Patroklos, *Patroklus athla*. This subject, developed in book XXIII of the *Iliad*, is taken up with some variation, as we have seen, on the neck of the François vase: between the legs of the horses which rush forward appear the tripods which were given to the winners. *Athlon, athla:* the event and the prize are but one. In this archaic culture athleticism has for its main meaning not the surpassing of oneself but the victory over the other: one must be the best.

The term *athlon* has a synonym – *agôn* – whose semantic range goes beyond that of physical exercise. This word also designates an assembly, whatever it may be, just as much as the competition itself. The antagonists confront each other under the gaze of the spectators, similar to the way one witnesses the verbal confrontations of the protagonists in the theatre, in a type of dialogue also called *agôn*.

Aside from these competitions, the athletes exercise in special places set aside for such practice: the palaestra and the gymnasium. *Palaiô* signifies to wrestle, and the place *palaistra* identifies itself with the activity which occurs there. *Gymnos* signifies nudity or undress. The nudity of athletes is a trait specific to the archaic and classical Greek world, and to that of Athens in particular. Thucydides, at the beginning of his history, in evoking the Greek past, points out that the Athenians "were also the first who showed themselves nude and who, appearing in public without clothes, rubbed themselves down with oil in the competitions. In the past, even for competing in Olympic events

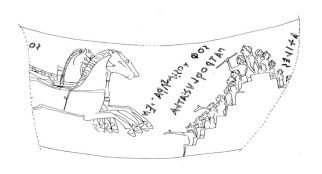

52. ATTIC BLACK-FIGURE DINOS, SOPHILOS
580 BC, PRESERVED HEIGHT 0.15 M
ATHENS, ARCHAEOLOGICAL MUSEUM

1. Thucydides, *The Peloponnesian War,* 1,6,5.

(en toi olympikoi agoni), the athletes wore a sort of belt which hid their genitals; it was a few years ago that this stopped."[1]

Nudity, then, becomes a typically Greek characteristic whose importance in the visual domain is considerable. In terms of sculpture or vase painting, the nudity of young athletes occupies a remarkable place in the figurative repertoire.

One is aware of the radical transformation which took effect in the history of vase techniques towards the end of the 6th century BC, at the time of the change from black figures to red figures. The chromatic relationship between figure and back-ground is reversed. The characters, up to then painted in black silhouette on the red clay background, were henceforth screened in red on a background glazed in black. The particulars of the design also changed: in black-figure painting, it is carved into the clay surface; in red-figure painting, it is a painted line, a more or less thick stroke which gains suppleness and delicacy in relation to the rigidity of the engraved line. It has often been noted that the new technique of red-figure painting allowed a more subtle rendering of anatomy, particularly that of athletes. It would be difficult and certainly absurd to seek to determine the cause and the effect, to pretend that the invention of red-figure painting had as a consequence the multiplication of athletic scenes, or inversely that the interest in athletes brought about an evolution towards red-figure painting. One notes in any case a remarkable development of this theme around the years 520-510 BC, in particular in the generation of painters which one calls the Pioneers of red-figure painting.

The work surrounding the representation of the body, of the musculature and of postures in tension or in movement, seems to have had a great hold on those painters who multiplied their graphic researches and experimented with new solutions. More than in scenes of competition, they were interested in the postures of athletes in training, and in their gymnastic activity under the gaze of the trainers and judges.

The scenes of exercise therefore became a frequent spectacle on the vases, for the pleasure of the drinkers who used them; they echo the verses of Theognis: "Happy the lover who frequents the gymnasium *(gymnazetai)* to return home each day to sleep with a handsome young man *(sun kaloi paidi)*."[2]

An amphora in the Louvre attributed to one of these Pioneers, Phintias, and whose decor of framing borrows from the two techniques at the same time – palm leaves in black-figure on the bottom and on

53. 53. ATTIC RED-FIGURE AMPHORA, PHINTIAS
520-510 BC, HEIGHT 0.65 M
PARIS, LOUVRE

▶▶ **54.** DETAIL OF VASE, FIGURE 53.

2. Theognis, *Elegies,* 1335-36.

55. REVERSE OF VASE, FIGURE 53.

the sides, and red-figure on the upper portion of the picture – presents three athletes in training, under the gaze of a bearded adult. The latter, draped in his *himation,* staff in hand, stands immobile. The two athletes in the center of the image are beardless, with large shoulders and powerful thighs. One carries a discus on his shoulder. The other, body facing front, prepares his javelin, and his abdominal muscles are carefully detailed. A second javelin thrower, bearded, closes the image on the right. All the characters are crowned, which emphasizes their beauty and suggests that the competition, the festival in honor of the gods, is not far away. Finally, a series of inscriptions clarifies certain aspects of the representation; each figure is accompanied by a vertically inscribed name: *Sosias, Demostrate, Chares,* and *Sotinos.* But one also reads between the legs of one of the javelin throwers the word *chaire,* "hello," which is addressed as much to the figures represented as to the viewer of the image. Above this scene, horizontally, runs another expression of praise, *Sostratos kalos,* where one finds again the adjective *kalos,* which characterizes many of these archaic scenes.

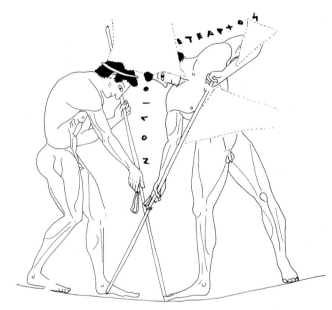

56. DETAIL OF AN ATTIC RED-FIGURE PSYKTER, PHINTIAS
520-510 BC, HEIGHT 0.24 M
BOSTON, MUSEUM OF FINE ARTS

The reverse of this amphora appears unrelated to the athletic scene. One sees Tityus between Artemis and Apollo trying to lift up Leto. Apollo tries to intervene to protect his mother. Tityus the giant behaves like a wrestler. He has lifted Leto up from the ground and holds her tightly so that it seems nothing could free her. It is violence of an athletic type which is practiced here, but in a mythological and erotic context.

Phintias is attentive to the movement of bodies and to the complexity

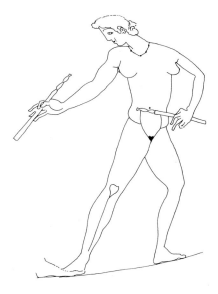

57. ATTIC RED-FIGURE AMPHORA, KLEOPHRADES PAINTER

500 BC, HEIGHT 0.63 M

WURZBURG UNIVERSITY

▶ **58.** ATTIC RED-FIGURE AMPHORA, NEAR THE KLEOPHRADES PAINTER

490 BC, HEIGHT 0.43 M

VIENNA, KUNSTHISTORISCHES MUSEUM

of the intertwined limbs, and of the musculature in tension. From this point of view, the frontal figure of the young javelin thrower is striking: torso facing front, right arm and leg stretched to the side, and on the other side arm and leg bent. One finds this posture again, barely modified, on a *psykter* attributed to the same painter. The athlete, named *Etearchos,* leans in the same way, and one understands his gesture better thanks to the neighboring figures: each javelin is propelled with the help of a strap wrapped around the middle of the pole. On the *psykter* one clearly sees the loop which forms this strap which is not yet wound around the javelin of his companion named *Philon.*

The technical gesture allows one to emphasize the beauty of the bodies of the athletes. These young men are beautiful and their malleability forms a sort of canon, an absolute model, to the point that when the painters of this period were brought to represent a naked woman, they gave her a male body. Women were rarely without clothing, except at their bath or in erotic scenes of the *comos* and the banquet. On an amphora attributed to the Kleophrades painter, who is closely related to the Pioneers, an *aulos* player who accompanies the drinkers is nude. Her body, seen from the front, is constructed like that of the javelin thrower: her high breasts perched under her arms are tacked onto the torso of an athlete with very muscular hips. The painter does not reveal here his inability to render the female anatomy: it is simply the masculine body which is the more desirable model.

This body is so perfect that it is sufficient in itself. An amphora by the same Kleophrades painter shows an isolated athlete on each side. No other figure accompanies the character who is emphasized in this way: no exercise companion, no trainer, no spectator. Nothing frames the image; the body stands out against the background of black glaze without even a line for the ground upon which to stand.

On one side the athlete, leaning slightly, washes himself with a strigil; on the other, a boxer, head tilted, adjusts on his wrist a long leather strap *(himantes)* designed to strengthen the blows during the match. On both surfaces, it is not only the body of the athlete which holds the attention of the painter, but more precisely the bodily needs to which he devotes himself: his grooming and his technical preparation. This fixation upon the image of beauty comes before the representation of the event itself. The attitude of the pugilist, in his quasi-statuesque isolation, adapts remarkably well to the form of the vase itself. The elbows which stand out from the torso echo the handles, and the

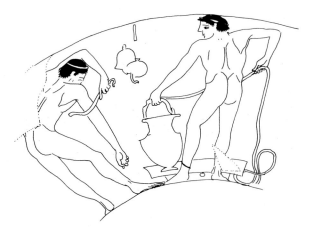

shoulders spreading wide at the top echo the shoulder of the vase. And so, one might say, the athlete is the vase made flesh.

This attention paid to grooming, to preparations and to the representation of the youthful body is found not only in the production of the red-figure Pioneers, but in the following generations, up to the end of the archaic period, particularly with cup painters.

Onesimos, on a vase in the Louvre, has multiplied the points of view from which the bathing athletes are seen. The exterior of the vase, which is incomplete, shows on one side three young men around a stone basin *(louterion)*, and on the other three athletes around a well. The central character draws the water which will serve to fill the basin, while the others hold strigils and scrape their skin. Four among them are seen from behind, the group forming a series of variations on the motif of the back of the body. The medallion, on the other hand, represents a young man facing front. Not only his body, but his face is frontal, which is rare in vase painting where the figures are almost always in profile. This frontality implicates the viewer of the image in a *vis-à-vis* which accentuates the game of gazes and desire.

The young man leans his head; he squeezes a sponge above a basin of bronze upon which one reads, once again, the inscription *kalos* – "handsome." The word describes both the grooming and the figure represented at the same time. In the background to the right, is a pair of sandals; to the left, a staff and a pack in which one recognizes a scraper with a swan-neck handle, as well as a small perfume vase, a completely round aryballos with its strap hanging. All the grooming accessories are spread out in the space around the young man who gazes at us. Near his head one reads the verb *erchetai,* "he comes." Without a doubt this announces the arrival of a person from outside the image. It is difficult to further specify the meaning of this inscription because it is without equivalent; but it is clear that we have here a fragment of a dialogue which, together with the front-facing aspect of the speaker, implicates us in the scene. The young man is handsome and the drinker takes pleasure in gazing at him head on in the bottom of the cup, while in turning the cup to the exterior, he will see athletes from behind.

The spectacle of bodies multiplied on the banquet vases is one of the essential dimensions of archaic visual culture, in the world of vase painting as well as that of sculpture.

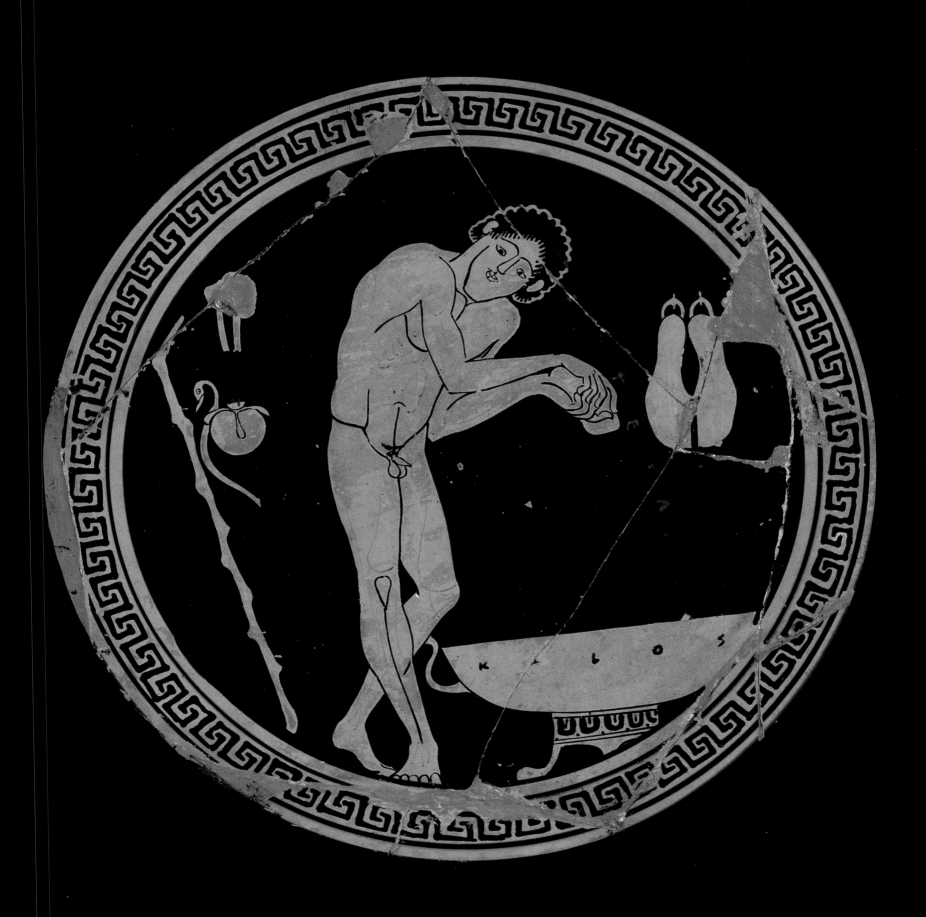

▶ **61.** ATTIC RED-FIGURE CUP, KISS PAINTER
500 BC, DIAMETER 0.30 M
BALTIMORE, JOHNS HOPKINS UNIVERSITY

On a cup in Baltimore, one observes an interesting shift between these two worlds of painting and sculpture. To the left, an adult wearing a crown and a *himation,* with staff in hand, stands before a young victorious athlete, who is shown on a sort of podium, or *bêma,* which elevates him like a statue on its base. Crowned, he holds a javelin in his right hand, and in his left a pack – sponge and aryballos – similar to the one which is suspended in the background of the image. In front of the base is planted a pickaxe for loosening the soil. The young victor with powerful thighs is seen in profile, but his torso is presented head-on, mostly displayed toward the viewer. While the anatomic rendering here loses exactness, the expressive force of the athletic body becomes evident. Here again the inscriptions which accompany the image prolong and go beyond the contents of the representation. One reads, moving out from the head of the adult, two words: in front of him *Leagros* and behind *kalos,* "Leagros is beautiful." This name does not necessarily designate, as has been claimed, the figure of the young victor; one finds it again on a number of other vases and sometimes in scenes where no young man appears (cf. chap. 1). The praise of Leagros does not directly apply to the figure of the young athlete, but rather echoes him.

But how to understand this figure? Is it about an athlete, or is it about his statue? The aestheticization of the victorious body may just as easily lead to the representation of his activity as to the creation, on the vase, of an image of the image, which takes upon itself all the plastic values which are made visible by the sculpture.

Pausanias, a traveler in Greece in the 2nd century AD, reminds us, in describing the monuments of Olympia, that the athletes victorious at the games had the right to consecrate, in thanks to the gods, as many statues as their victories brought them. Pliny states precisely regarding the uses of bronze: "It was customary to reproduce only the image of men who merited immortality through some act of renown; at first they were the victors of the sacred games, especially in Olympia, where it was customary to dedicate a statue to all those who had won a victory; for those who triumphed three times, one would erect statues made according to nature: one calls the statues of this type iconic *(statuas...ex membris ipsorum similitudine expressa, quas iconicas vocant)."* [3]

The statue was thus like a votive object with religious value, since it was offered to the gods after a victory that was owing to them, and also

3. Pliny the Elder, *Natural History,* XXXIV, 9, 16.

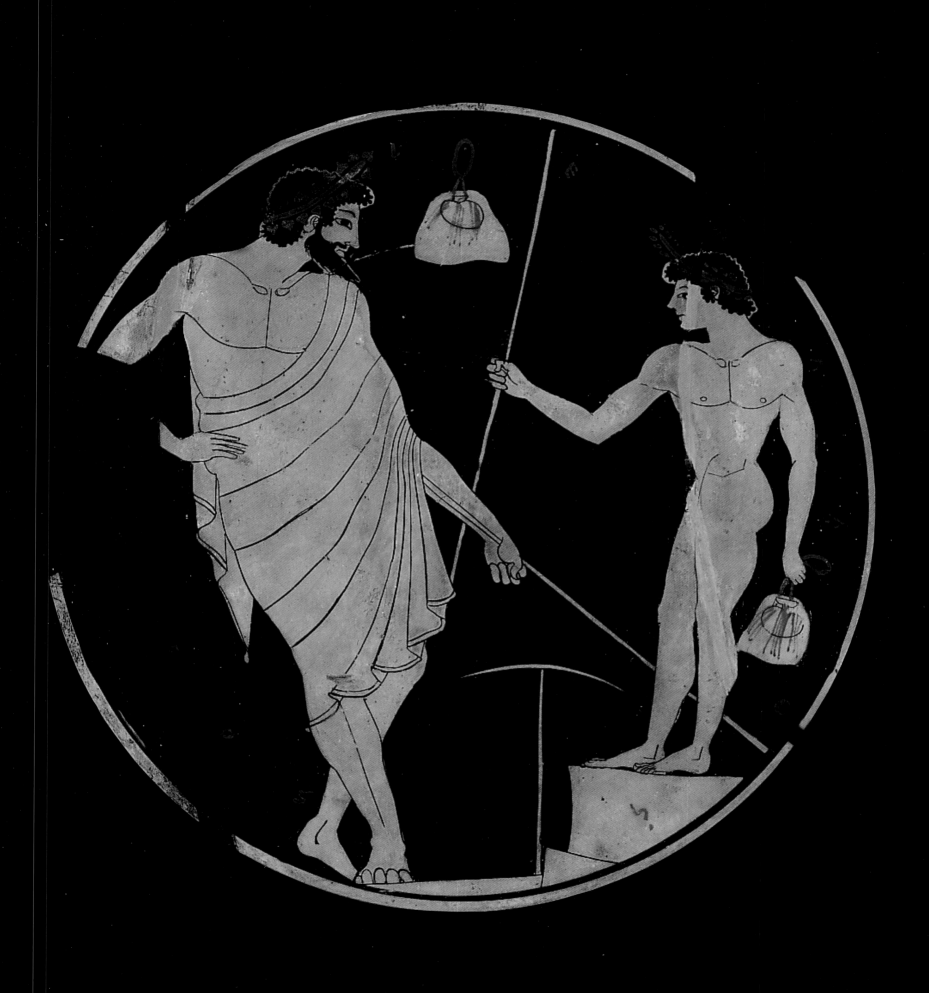

as a monument which perpetuated this victory and proclaimed it forever in the public space of the temple. Glory and piety, then, make a pair. The aesthetic dimension of the statue is only, in this context, one of the components of the work. Pliny clarifies that it is the faithfulness to the anatomy of the victor which gives it the quality of an icon and not the resemblance of the facial characteristics, which would have made it a portrait, which did not yet exist in the archaic period in the sense that we understand it. Only the inscription specifies the identity of the victor in naming him.

On the Baltimore cup, all the values connected with archaic statuary are implicitly present, but put back in a different context. *Epidromos kalos* is named on the exterior, just as *Leagros* on the medallion. The exterior of the vase represents comasts around a krater: a group of drinkers making merry, quite possibly in honor of a victorious athlete, but in a private way, among friends. We are not in the temple of Zeus in Olympia, or the Agora in Athens, where we meet the statues dedicated to the gods in thanks for victory, but at a private banquet, among citizens who take pleasure in admiring the beautiful athletes.

Is the young man on the medallion upon his podium a victor, or are we before his statue? Must we even decide? The purpose of the image is precisely to suggest by the graphic copy a quasi-total equivalence between the beauty of the athlete and his iconic counterpart.

Plato, at the beginning of *Charmides,* shows a Socrates who, returning to Athens after the battle of Potidea, is informed of the news and sees the beautiful young Charmides arrive: "All gaze upon him as if he were the statue of a god. At this, Cherephon questions me: 'Socrates,' he said to me, 'how do you find this youth? Has he not a handsome face? – Unbelievably handsome,' I responded. – 'Ah, but if,' he replied, 'he agreed to undress, his face would count for nothing, since the beauty of his shape is perfect.'"[4]

Athletic nudity and the statuary which immortalizes it establish, as we have seen, the norms of aesthetic judgement. The young Charmides is beautiful like a god, but only the statue can claim to preserve without alteration the youth and the brilliance which, ephemeral in humans, are eternal with the gods.

The vase painters did not, like Socrates, limit themselves to taking a secret look at the beauty of athletes. Pottery in Athens held an official role at the time of the Panathenaia, where the victors received the

4. Plato, *Charmides,* 154 d-e.

sacred oil in amphoras whose decoration evoked the goddess as well as the event that was won.

The religious and public dimensions of the athletic competitions are essential in Greek culture. All the great meetings, all the *agones* which joined the best athletes are associated with the temples and take place in honor of the gods. In Olympia (the most important of the panhellenic sanctuaries, shared by all the Greeks) one honors Zeus, and the victors are crowned with olive branches. In Nemea, as well, the games are played in honor of Zeus, but the crown is made of wild celery. At Delphi, Apollo presides over the Pythian Games, and the crown is laurel. And finally, near Corinth, in the Isthmus, the games take place for Poseidon, and they win a crown of pine.

These four major places form the quadrennial cycle of the great, most prestigious games. In Athens every four years the Great Panathenaian Games are celebrated in honor of the goddess who gave her name to the city. This festival falls the third year of each olympiad, in the month of July, and lasts at least four days. All sorts of events are played, athletic and musical alike. The main event, in Athens and elsewhere, is the chariot race. In the funeral games organized by Achilles in honor of Patroklos, such as are recalled in the *Iliad*,[5] it is the event described at the most length, and it is also the one which figures on the lower register on the neck of the François vase (fig. 1 and 74).

The prestige earned by such a victory reflects more on the owner of the chariot and his city of origin than on the chariot driver. Such glory, in order to fix itself in the memory of men, needs artists and poets, and it is through them that we have kept track of these exploits. Pindar in particular specialized in these odes composed on command and sung during the triumphant return of the victors to their city. The editors in Alexandria classified these poems according to the competitions to which they referred: the *Olympic, Pythian, Isthmian,* and *Nemean* odes.

In an ode in honor of Theaios of Argos, winner at wrestling, Pindar recalls the earlier victories of this athlete and alludes to the vases which he won at Athens: "Twice before, as happy prelude, the Athenians in their solemn festivals accompanied him with their sweet acclamations and he brought back to the valiant people of Hera the fruit of the olive branch within the sides of the richly decorated vases which the flame has hardened."[6]

These richly decorated vases *(pampoikiloi)* must have been produced in considerable quantities, from the middle of the 6th up to the 4th

5. Homer, *Iliad,* xxiii, 257-897.

6. Pindar, *Nemean Odes,* 10, 33-36.

century BC. We know of nearly 300 of them, all the same type and all maintaining, even at an advanced date, the black-figure painting technique. These amphoras, nicknamed panathenaic by archaeologists, have a large belly and a narrow neck and foot, which recalls the shape of ordinary storage amphoras. From the end of the 5th century BC, the type is standardized; one constantly finds the image of Athena between two columns, an inscription indicating the origin of the vase – *ton atheneten athlon,* "one of the prizes from Athens" – and, on the reverse, a scene bringing to mind one of the events of the games: running, wrestling, jumping, boxing, etc.

An amphora of this type, discovered in the necropolis of Camiros on Rhodes, belongs to the beginning of this series, around 550 BC. On the main side towers the image of the armed Athena; she brandishes her spear and protects herself with a round shield decorated with a tripod; she wears a helmet and has on her chest an aegis covered with scales and trimmed with serpents. The attitude of the goddess evokes the statuary type of Athena Promachos, or warrior. On either side, two masculine figures of small stature, wearing crowns, similar to the *kouroi* of archaic sculpture, advance while holding long branches, offerings of plants intended for the goddess. The ritual character of the scene is emphasized by an original border, typical of this panathenaic series: two columns topped here by bronze cauldrons mark the limits of the field of the image around the goddess. These cauldrons, as well as the tripod which appears on the shield of Athena, bring to mind the prizes won by the athletes and the offerings consecrated to the gods. As for the columns, they suggest a sort of *temenos,* a kind of consecrated space into which the divine presence may enter, a presence who is both the object of the festival and the guarantor of the prestige conferred by the prize.

On the reverse side appears an astonishing scene, exceptional more for the presence of spectators than for the nature of the event portrayed. On the left of the scene stands the audience, seated on steps forming three levels; one of the spectators, body facing front, is foreshortened; a smaller individual is naked and stands on the last step. All are turned towards the right and encourage the athlete with voice and gesture. The direction of their gaze and of their outstretched arms is extended by a long inscription which crosses the field of the image at an angle, visually joining the athlete to the onlookers who cheer him. It is rare for the crowd to be so much a part of the image and to be within the view of the spectator. But this collective and playful dimension is an integral part of the pleasure of the games, as we see once again in the exemplary passage from the *Iliad,* during the funeral of Patroklos. The public stirs and participates in the spectacle by encouraging the competitors. Here the inscription conveys their enthusiasm: *kados tôi kubistetôi,* "the vase for the jumper."[7] The prize is thus awarded by the applause for the man who jumps on the back of a horse, carried away by the music of the *aulos*. One sees a musician standing before a sort of trapezoidal springboard. To the right a young cavalier waits, holding a second horse which is barely visible in the image (but the doubling of the hooves indicates the presence of another mount). A helmeted warrior, equipped with two shields, jumps on the hindquarters of this horse while turning, like his associate, towards the public. The motif which decorates his two shields, a series of concentric crescents, accentuates the twirling effect of the exercise. Placed at such a height, above the eyes of the spectators, this armed acrobat is of reduced size, not because his role is minor but because the pictorial space is not set out in a homogenous and proportional manner. Two other small-sized individuals bustle about around the horses; one loosens the ground with a pickaxe, the other balances himself up high on a sort of mast which is without doubt part of the accessories of the event.

It is difficult to say of what this consists exactly. Even if the inscription indicates that it has to do with a jump, one is reduced to conjectures which it matters little to detail here: perhaps this is a horse race with relay and jump, or even the competition of skill and bodily beauty called *euandria,* the "handsome men."

If this single image evokes an event which is for us enigmatic, the typology of the vase, its reverse side having an armed Athena between two columns, conforms to that which would in the 5th and 4th centuries BC become the panathenaic model.

Parallel to this class of vases which was ritually fixed and probably produced under the control of the organizing magistrates of the Panathenaian Games, there exist other vases which take up, be it in their form or in a part of their decoration, certain aspects of these official vases, thus appropriating something of the prestige of the great Athenian festival.

7. Others read *kalos tôi kubistetôi,* "bravo for the jumper," making *kalos* an adverb; but the third letter is a D not an L.

63. REVERSE OF VASE, FIGURE 62

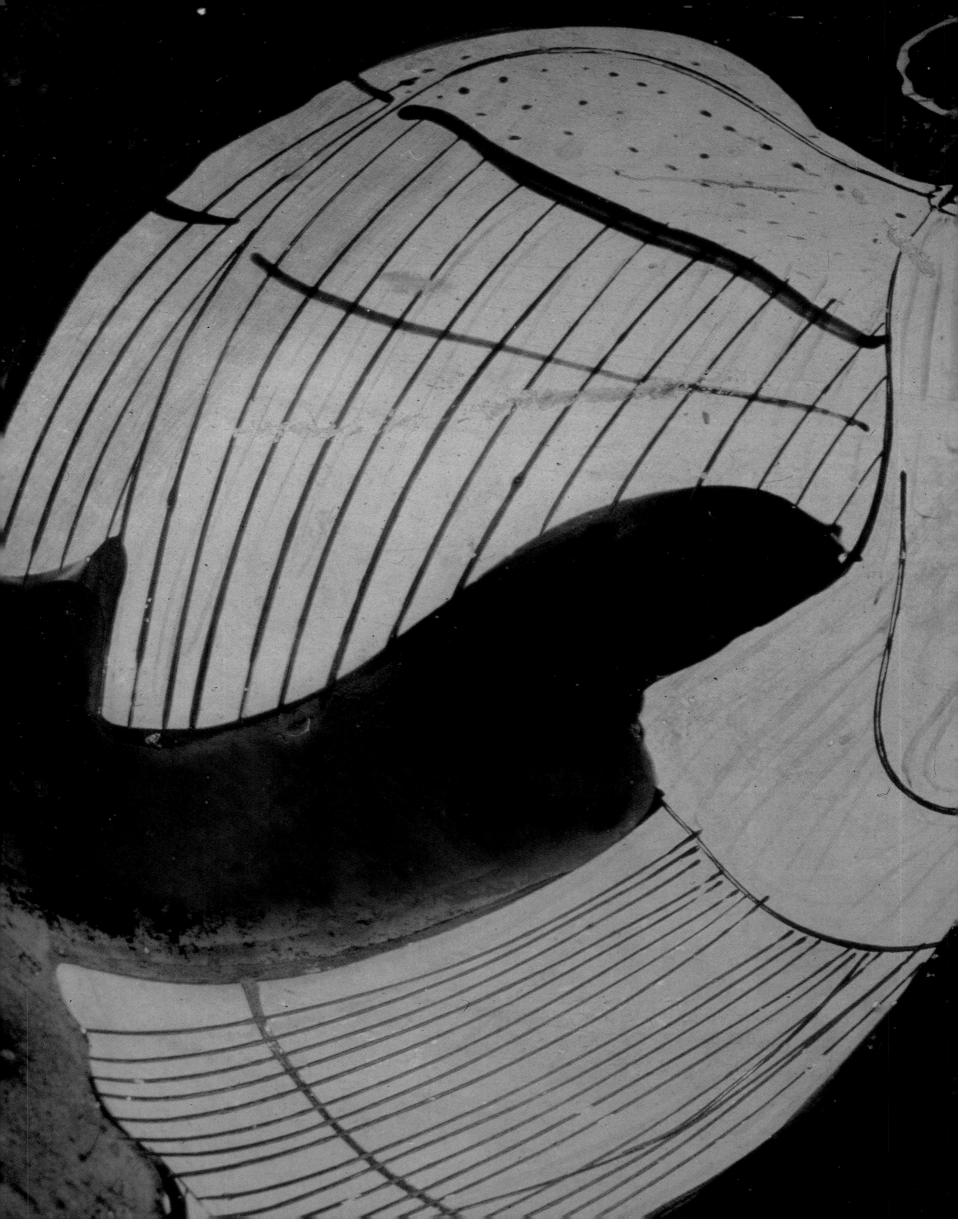

This is the case with an amphora of a common type called a neck amphora, upon which there is a musician; he is dressed in a long chiton and plays the cithara: there is a plectrum, or pick, in his right hand, and his left hand is behind the strings. A piece of fabric hangs from the resonance chamber; it is the cover which protects the strings when the instrument is not being used.

The cithara is the instrument of singers, of bards, and of professional musicians; it differs from the lyre in size, weight, and the technical virtuosity which it requires. The musicians use it in musical competitions and the frame which the painter uses here, two columns topped with cocks, suggests the Panathenaic Games, except that it is not Athena but a cithara player who is inscribed in this space. One could also think of Apollo, the musician god; without doubt the image plays upon this ambiguity, which we find again in other representations. The musician, like the athlete, has something of the god about him.

The place reserved in the games for music is considerable, with the exception of those in Olympia. Not only does it accompany athletic exercises, as we have seen with the jumper and his two shields, and as has been seen in the armed dance known as the Pyrrhic (which is said to have been invented by Athena herself), but it occupies a part of the program of the competitions. This would not have been surprising in Delphi, at the temple of Apollo, master of the Muses, the cithara player *par excellence*. Nor is Athena a stranger to music; she is credited with the invention of the *aulos,* that sort of oboe with which she imitates the wail of the Gorgons crying over the death of the decapitated Medusa.

While the importance of music is evident in archaic culture, not only at the banquet but also in the contests, the details of the competitions escape us. An inscription from the 4th century BC indicates that at the Panathenaian Games there took place a cithara song contest (singing accompanied by the cithara), an *aulos* song contest (singing accompanied by someone playing the *aulos*), and an *aulos* contest (an instrumental solo). It is by these songs produced at the time of the musical competitions that there entered into the collective memory the epic and the narratives of the age of gods and heroes, such as are found pictured on temples and vases.

Outside the strict frame of the Panathenaian Games, many images allude to the musical contests where the cithara holds an emblematic role. One sees this instrument in the hands of a Nike on an amphora which is today in Vienna. This female winged figure in flight does not play the cithara but presents the instrument as a sign of poetic and musical activity. On the reverse stands a young man draped with material, perhaps the recipient of the cithara, the triumphant musician. Nike, the personification of Victory, takes here her full meaning; she indicates the favor of the gods and success in the competition, whatever it may be. The vase has nothing Panathenaian about it and the context of this victory is not specified. But one notices that the image, more than representing the competition, makes visible that which has been sought by all: Victory, the success sent by the gods, to whom one must give thanks. Before the face of this divine figure one reads the word *kalos,* and, along the embroidered material which hangs from the cithara the name *Timonides.* Once again we find the classic formula: acclaim for a handsome young man who is not necessarily the one who appears on the other side.

The beauty of the young men and musical victory: the two are linked. One cannot separate in the presentation of imagery by the vase painters that which extols bodily beauty from that which concerns musical pleasure and poetic recitation. These are two faces of a single culture, of the body and of the spirit.

On the François vase, Theseus, the leader of a group of young people, holds a lyre (fig. 11). The exploit of a young hero is not inconsistent with musical activity. Similarly, in the *Iliad,* when Achilles renounces taking part in combat because he feels himself unjustly treated by Agamemnon, he sulks in his tent and plays the cithara: "His heart was pleased to play the sonorous cithara…while he sang the exploits of heroes. Alone, facing him, Patroklos sits in silence." [8]

This is a curious scene, in which a hero sings of the heroes of the past. But this self-reflective playing should not be surprising. The glory of Achilles is nothing without a Homer to sing it; in the collective memory, the epic song serves as a relay in the transmission of the exploits of the past.

The close tie which one observes in the framework of the games between athletic events and musical contests calls attention to the same social logic: in reciting the *Iliad* at the Panathenaia, the rhapsodizing poets revive the epic memory of the Athenian people, who in turn celebrate the physical virtues of strength and beauty, which are found in the hero as well as the athlete.

8. Homer, *Iliad,* 9, 189-90.

WARRIORS AND HEROES 4

▶ **66.** ATTIC BLACK-FIGURE AMPHORA, PAINTER OF BERLIN 1686
540 BC, HEIGHT 0.38 M
PARIS, CABINET DES MÉDAILLES, BIBLIOTHÈQUE NATIONALE

Although the sculptors decorating the temples were interested in the great mythical battles, those of gods against giants, and those of Greeks against Amazons and against centaurs, the vase painters seemed more interested in the image of the warrior as a heroic figure captured in isolation.

Of course they did not ignore the themes of the archaic repertoire and one could easily compare a certain vase by Lydos with the frieze of the Siphnian treasury at Delphi. However, they very quickly concentrated their attention on certain individual aspects of the warrior's activity and thus focused their own particular gaze on war at the level of the warrior.

In this respect, a black figure amphora found in Vulci combines on its two sides many characteristic aspects. On one side, one witnesses the preparations for departure. The painting, which includes many individuals, can be divided into two scenes which are usually independent. To the left a naked bearded warrior stands on his right leg; leaning forward, he fits his left leg with a bronze shin-protector, a cnemid. At his feet lies the rest of his armor: a large round shield and a helmet decorated with three plumes which look like a crest. This warrior is framed by two figures; a hoary old man to the left, and to the right a long-haired woman who holds his sword out to him. The figures thus form a sort of family group in which he who is going to leave is surrounded by those who will remain in the domestic space, the *oikos*. While one can without doubt consider that the old man is the father of the warrior, it is difficult to say exactly who is the woman with the sword. Is she the wife or the mother of the soldier who arms himself? She seems young, or at least ageless; the contrast of young and old, relevant for men because it determines an ability to bear arms, for women means nothing in this context. In other images of the same type where mythic figures are named, this woman is the mother of the hero, Hecuba in front of Hector, and not his wife Andromache.

On this amphora the painter sought to inscribe some of the names; one can see a series of letters along the raised leg of the warrior. But these well-formed letters, arranged all over the vase, make no sense. One often finds this phenomenon during this period, in the second half of the 6th century BC. This purely ornamental use of the letter can be surprising: it has nothing to do with naming the figures, but rather with urging the viewer to verbally formulate their name. The inscription functions not as a key explaining the image, but as the opening mechanism of the story, activating the memory of the viewer.

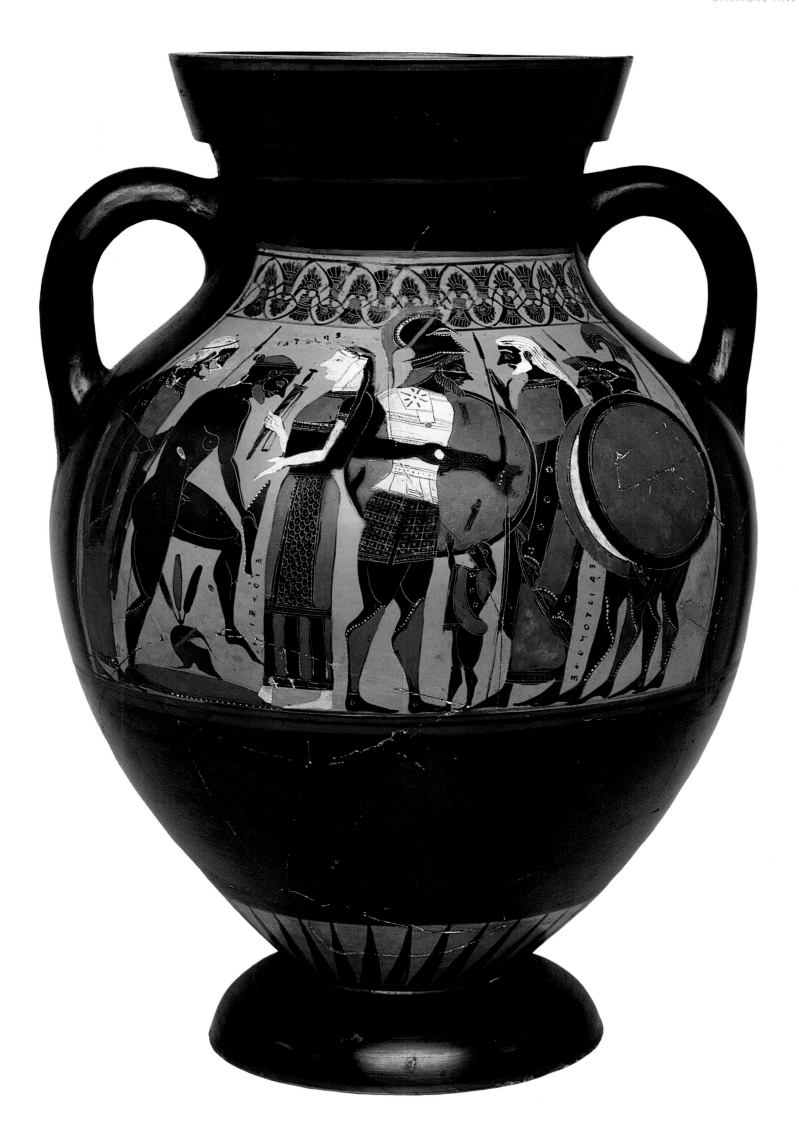

In short, the viewer does not read the image, he recognizes it.

For us in modern times, who are not immediately disposed to this method of recognition, this method of collective memory which is characteristic of archaic Greek culture, it is often difficult to name with certainty the figures represented. On the entire vase, one comes up against a kind of uncertainty. It has been suggested that we see here Thetis in front of Achilles, or Helen in front of Paris, but these are suppositions; it seems clear, however, that the painter wanted to point us towards the epic and heroic world where the figures have fame, a *kleos,* and a proper name.

The right part of the painting represents another group of warriors, in a scene of leave-taking. In the center an old man with a white beard is followed by two hoplites whose red and white shields create by their superimposition an effect of depth. Before him stands another hoplite, in a white breastplate. In his right hand he holds an unfooted cup of finely worked metal, a phiale which serves in libations. This object is in itself the ritual sign of the bond which joins the figures together: in making a libation to the gods, that is to say in pouring in their honor a bit of liquid that they then drink in turn, humans symbolically mark the relationships which unite them and the protection of the gods whom they invoke at the moment of leaving for combat.

◄ **67**. REVERSE OF THE AMPHORA, FIGURE 66

The donning of armor and the departure for war are thus joined in a single painting. The two old men and the woman, as well as the child who stands in front of the old man facing the hoplite who holds the phiale, under his large shield, are among the members of the household, those who do not go away. More than the exploits of the warrior, it is the intimate and private moment of departure which holds the attention of the painter.

On the other side is a battle scene, or more precisely, a duel. Here, one encounters again an example of putting things in focus. The painters seem to prefer scenes which emphasize an individual exploit, and the singularity of a heroic encounter, to the generalized fray and the furor of the pitched battle. In this their choice conforms to the epic model; the *Iliad* gives more space to great duels which demonstrate the bravery of this or that hero, as well as his superiority, his *aristeia,* than to obscure battles which are there only to serve as the backdrop to great epic moments.

On this vase, the duel turns to the advantage of the warrior on the left. His adversary defends himself with difficulty; one knee on the ground, he seems already to be moving away or fleeing, and his movement is

68. DETAIL OF THE SHOULDER
ATTIC BLACK-FIGURE AMPHORA, FIGURES 143 AND 166
AMASIS PAINTER, 540 BC, HEIGHT 0.32 M
PARIS, CABINET DES MÉDAILLES, BIBLIOTHÈQUE NATIONALE

emphasized by the flight of a bird between the legs of the attacker. The scene is framed by two women whose gestures of victory and panic comment upon the scene.

From a "realistic" perspective, these women obviously have no place on a battlefield. But their presence refers to a pattern in the epic which bears out the false inscriptions. These are the mothers of the heroes in battle, perhaps Thetis and Aurora, next to Achilles and Memnon, or Aphrodite watching over Aeneas; the image does not allow an answer and suggests only unspecified epic themes.

There exist many more scenes of duels than of mass battles. On an amphora representing the gods (fig. 143, 166), the Amasis painter has taken up this motif once more, multiplying it to create an ornamental frieze which better evokes the masses of men in group combat. But even in this case, the care given to the detailed account of the motifs which decorate the shields shows that the brilliance of arms and the bravery of the individual are favored to the detriment of the more somber and dramatic aspects of combat.

In concentrating upon the individualizing aspects of war – armor, leave-taking, goodbyes to the family – the painters have also developed a rare but revealing motif, that of divination.

▶ **69.** ATTIC BLACK-FIGURE AMPHORA, ANTIMENES PAINTER
520 BC, HEIGHT 0.41 M
BOULOGNE-SUR-MER, CHÂTEAU MUSÉE

One finds a good example of this on an amphora attributed to the Antimenes painter. The scene is composed of only three characters: an old man, a hoplite, and a young boy dressed in a simple loincloth tied at his waist who presents a large purplish mass, the liver of a sacrificial victim. The hoplite examines this liver with the tips of his fingers, to see

70. INTERIOR OF ATTIC RED-FIGURE CUP

PISTOXENOS PAINTER

480-470 BC, DIAMETER 0.32 M

PARIS, LOUVRE

71, 72. EXTERIOR OF THE CUP, FIGURE 70

if the signs are favorable. The old man at the left extends his right hand over the young *pais*, to also point out to him the ritual spot for reading the signs. This examination of entrails consecrated to the gods *(hiera),* or more precisely of the liver of the victim (from which come the names *hieroscopy* or *hepatoscopy,* which are used for the ritual), has as its purpose the reading of divine signs. One does not seek to predict the future in its entirety, but simply to assure oneself that, with the decision to leave for war having been made, all will be well. The question is put in a binary form: "Is it, yes or no, a good time to leave," and not in an open-ended way: "What must I do?," or "What will happen?"

In this scene, the graphic economy accentuates the intensity of the divinatory procedure. The technique of carrying the liver, feeling it or marking it out, and the play of gazes concentrated on this focal point of the image, highlight the importance of this ritual inspection which is presented here as a key moment of the military life.

Generally, on banquet vases meant for private use – to distinguish them from those used in public memorials – the painters favored an individual and particular, quasi-familial point of view of the warrior. A cup attributed to the Pistoxenos painter gives us a remarkable example of the image of the horseman. On the medallion, a young man in Thracian boots and covered by a heavy cloak sits immobile, two lances in his hand, head uncovered, with a wide-brimmed hat fallen back on the nape of his neck. Above his head once again we read *kalos,* "he is handsome." This cup is dated around 470 BC and these are the same riders we find again, forty years later, prancing on the frieze of the Parthenon.

The exterior of the vase places this motif of the rider's departure in its proper context, that of the *oikos.* On a fragmented surface, the young man on foot leads his horse while a hoplite arms himself next to a woman who holds out to him a libation oinochoe, and an old man, standing and leaning on his staff, holds his left hand to his head, as a sign of affliction.

On the better-preserved obverse, a fully armed hoplite is seated before a woman who offers him a phiale for a libation. To the right a young man in a Thracian cloak caresses the head of his horse, stopped in front of a column, a sign of the domestic space which the hoplite and the rider prepare to leave. Next to the column a writing case seems to refer either to the enrollment of the cavaliers, the *dokimasia,* or to the well-read education of young men, as we have already been able to observe on the banquet cups.

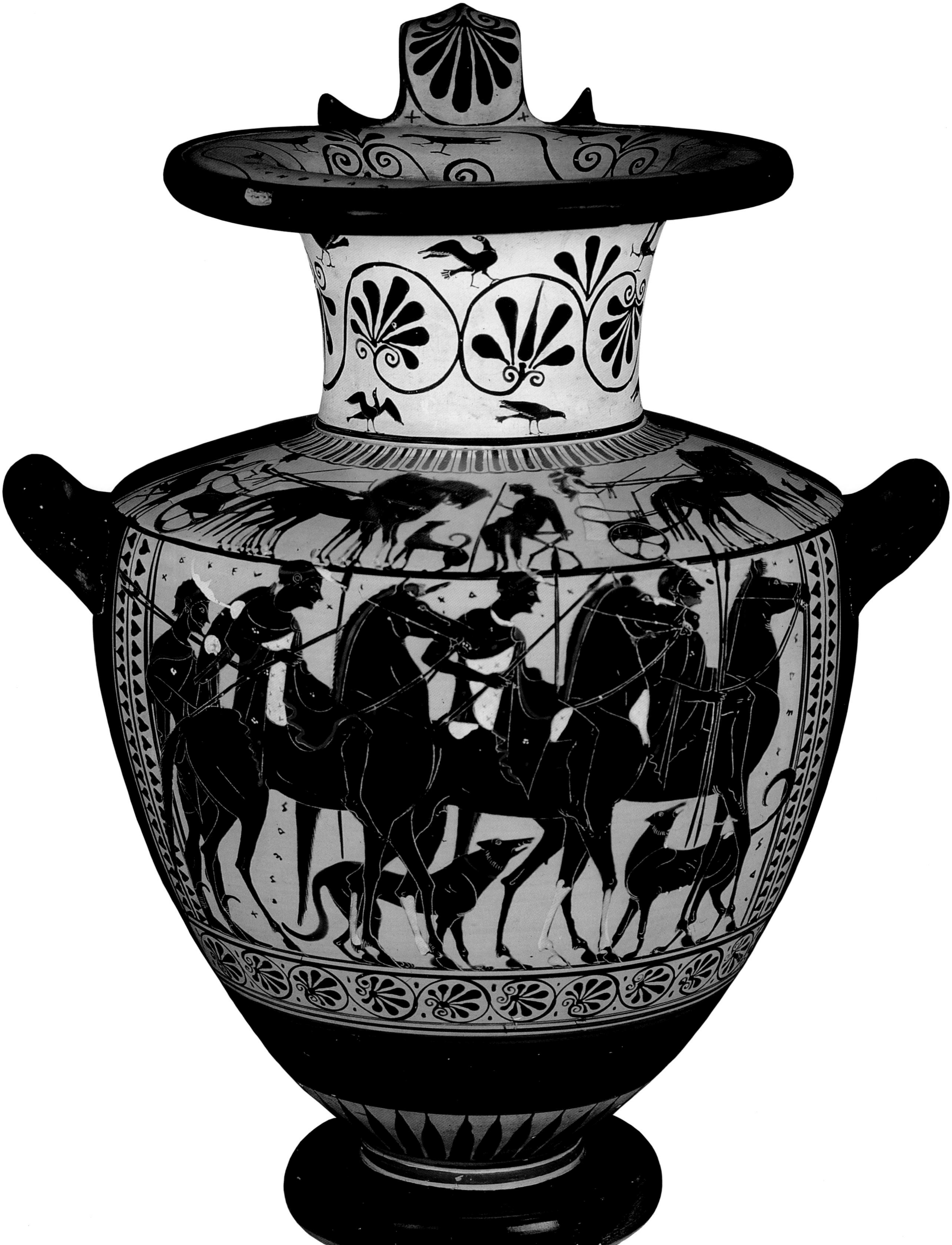

The Thracian dress of the cavaliers – the flapped boots, cloaks with crenellated motifs, fur hats – does not indicate an ethnic identity, which would have meant that these riders were Thracian barbarians in Athens. This kind of dress reveals a fashion; one which recognized in Thracians a particular skill in horsemanship, and one which the young Athenians claim for themselves. This elegance is emphasized by the inscriptions, as much on the medallion, as we have seen, as on the exterior of the vase, where we twice find the formula *ho pais kalos*. The cavalry of Athens constituted the most well-to-do class in their system of citizenship, and was often linked with the aristocracy in ancient times. Therefore it is not surprising to see that such a subject is often treated by the vase painters for the pleasure of the drinkers who are connected with this well-off class.

One finds the image of the riders again in another domain, one closely related to war, that of the hunt. On a hydria in the Louvre three horsemen ride past, followed by a figure on foot. All wear a flat hat, the *petasos,* and each have two lances whose play of verticals and angles regularly criss-crosses the painting; the third horseman has shifted his shield to his back, while the dogs which accompany them suggest the hunt. This scene belongs to a series in which the cavaliers who are followed by dogs never hunt, but only parade before our eyes. It is neither war nor the hunt which engage the painters, but the illustration of the youthful valor which justifies the distinction of the handsome Athenians: the prestige of the parade, the beauty of the march, the harmonious companionship of the young men – as much hunters as warriors. The elegance of the subject is confirmed here by the sophistication of the decoration. In an exceptional way, the neck of the vase as well as the interior of the mouth are not glazed black as is usual, but are covered by a white ground which leaves the field free for a series of palmettes inhabited by various birds painted in silhouette. The ornament comes to life, restoring a nature in harmony with the departure of the hunters.

The hunt is often the occasion of the exploits which prepare young men for the toughest encounters on the battlefield. In exercising simultaneously skill, cunning and strength, the hunt constitutes the drill *par excellence* of military apprenticeship. But it is also the place for all the dangers: the stories of the hunt are often dramatic, particularly in mythology. On the neck of the François vase, Meleager and his companions confront the enormous wild boar which ravages Calydon;

◀ **73.** ATTIC BLACK-FIGURE HYDRIA, NOT ATTRIBUTED
520 BC, HEIGHT 0.48 M
PARIS, LOUVRE

74. DETAIL OF NECK
ATTIC BLACK-FIGURE KRATER, CLITIAS
570 BC, HEIGHT 0.66 M
FLORENCE, ARCHAEOLOGICAL MUSEUM

this collective enterprise which brought together the elite of the heroic youth had a tragic outcome (cf. pp 15-16).

The distant, mountainous and wooded places where the hunter must track his game are not without dangers, and Artemis the huntress, the ferocious virgin goddess and mistress of animals, does not allow an easy approach. The story of Actaeon, with its tragic reversals, attests to this. The stories about this young Theban hunter vary. According to some, he tried to court his aunt Semele, and therefore brought upon himself the anger of Zeus. According to others, Euripides in particular, he boasted about being a better hunter than Artemis. And finally, according to still others, he saw Artemis bathing – just as Tiresias had surprised Athena. If the offence was the same, the punishment differed: Tiresias was blinded, while Actaeon was turned into game, either because Artemis transformed him into a deer and his own dogs attacked him, or because she sent the dogs into a blind fury and, no longer recognizing him, they devoured him.

On a krater in the Louvre, one sees a toppled Actaeon who desperately tries to defend himself against his pack of dogs while one of his companions flees, terrified. To the left, Artemis, immobile on her chariot harnessed with deer, and Apollo, near the rock which marks the center of the world, the *omphalos,* watch the scramble. Nothing turns Actaeon into a deer; his metamorphosis in this image, if it takes place, takes place only in the eyes of the dogs. To see and to be seen: had Actaeon not surprised Artemis, his dogs would not see him simply as game. The terrible impassiveness of the divine twins constructs, within the representation, the image of the viewer who witnesses the death of Actaeon, and warns him of the dangers of pride and indiscretion towards the gods.

From one vase to the other, from the parade of horsemen to the tragic hunt of Actaeon, the reference point is changed: one moves from real-life experience to a mythical image. This change of level permits the vase painters, like the epic and tragic poets, to rethink in the imagination the values of the social world.

The myth of Actaeon allows the questioning of the categories of the hunt (the relationships between man and animal, hunter and hunted, the value of cunning and of ambush) and of the experience that the drinker can have in it. In the same way the epic, which sings the exploits of the heroes and makes the gods act on them from behind the scenes, gives the poets, particularly in the *Iliad,* but the vase painters as well, an occasion to go beyond the scheme of reality and to represent on another level the values of war. In the epic, the particular heroism of such a matchless figure dominates the collective action and holds the attention of the painters.

The case of Achilles, the "best of the Achaeans" according to the Homeric formula, is exemplary from this point of view. We know him from the *Iliad,* which sings of his anger. But the painters, while taking up Homeric themes, developed still other episodes. One cannot overlook them and they will be taken up here on three particularly significant vases.

A *skyphos* attributed to the Brygos painter recaptures in its own way an episode which concludes the *Iliad:* the theme of the ransom of Hektor. One knows that Achilles, humbled by Agamemnon, has retired to his tent, far from the battles. Patroklos, faithful friend of Achilles, has borrowed his armor from him in order to drive back the Trojans. They, seeing the arrival of the one they believe to be Achilles, give up their ground. But Hektor kills Patroklos in a duel and strips him of the armor. Achilles then wishes to avenge his companion. His mother, the divine Thetis, obtains for him new equipment forged by Hephaistos. Achilles launches an assault on the Trojans, challenges Hektor on the battlefield, and kills him.

Here begins, beyond the heroic exploit, an episode which exceeds in fury anything that a Greek could imagine. Achilles decided to push his

75. ATTIC RED-FIGURE KRATER, PAINTER OF THE WOOLLY SATYRS
450 BC, HEIGHT 0.51 M
PARIS, LOUVRE
▶▶ 76. DETAIL OF KRATER, FIGURE 75

vengeance further and to defile the dead body of the Trojan hero. Rather than returning him to his own people so that they might mourn him and bury him as he deserved and as ritual requires, Achilles attaches the corpse to his chariot and drags it in the dust, bruising its flesh and disfiguring the heroic body. Even worse, he then abandons it without burial, leaving it to the dogs and the birds. In place of the ritual display of the body, washed and prepared in its own home, followed by the funeral procession which must take it from its home to the cemetery, Hektor received as his due only this ignoble treatment. Yet Zeus, sympathetic to the Trojans, protected this corpse and preserved it miraculously intact in spite of everything. But as long as the funeral of Patroklos was not celebrated, Achilles refused to return Hektor to his people.

On the Vienna vase, Achilles, stretched on a banquet bed, is in the process of feasting, knife in one hand, a slice of meat in the other. In front of the bed on a table are two metal phiales and long slabs of meat. On the ground, under the bed, is lodged the bloody corpse of Hektor, wrists tied, arms outstretched, eyes closed, his face to the ground. One is struck by the contrast between these two bodies on either side of the bed, one living, the other lifeless. It is rare that one sees the image of a guest eating meat; the insistent presence of this flesh in the hands of Achilles and on the table is not accidental; it makes obvious the horror of the scene. Around Achilles are displayed all his weapons: sword on the right, helmet and shield on the left, decorated with the grimacing face of a Gorgon. Tongue sticking out, with eyes open wide and face framed by serpents, she dominates the scene with her mortifying gaze. Even the decoration of the bed suggests in silhouette the confrontation of the heroes: a panther facing a bull creates a sort of metaphor for the combat where Hektor met his death.

On the left, a cortege approaches, led by Priam, the old king with white hair. He is followed by four porters, laden with the precious objects which constitute the ransom of Hektor: in succession there appear three stacked phiales and a hydria; then a hydria and a large bowl; then two flat baskets containing, without doubt, valuable fabrics. This collection of objects, drawn from the treasure of Priam, is brought in a procession a bit like the dowry of a bride. But here no girl is given in marriage. The exchange of goods is more dramatic: the father does not give his daughter, but comes to collect his dead son.

In the *Iliad,* Priam, arriving at the barracks of Achilles at the moment when Achilles is finishing his meal, demands to see his son.

77, 78. ATTIC RED-FIGURE SKYPHOS, BRYGOS PAINTER
490 BC, HEIGHT 0.25 M
VIENNA, KUNSTHISTORISCHES MUSEUM

79. ATTIC BLACK-FIGURE KRATER, DETAIL OF HANDLE
570 BC, HEIGHT 0.66 M
FLORENCE, ARCHAEOLOGICAL MUSEUM

1. *Iliad,* XXIV, 583.

2. *Iliad,* XXII, 370.

Achilles then, while he receives the ransom, has Hektor washed and anointed, and then orders that he be wrapped in a finely-woven tunic, and that the body remain out of Priam's sight.[1]

In the picture, the representation of the bodies is totally different. The composition organizes the relationship between the protagonists in a startling manner. Priam stands upright before Achilles, who turns his gaze towards a young servant. Hektor is immediately visible, face down under the bed of Achilles. In this scene which expresses the tension between the sorrow of Priam who has come to humble himself before the murderer of his son, and the pride of Achilles, merciless avenger of the death of Patroklos, the quality of the drawing gives a noble appearance to the corpse of Hektor. In spite of its desecration, the body remains full of youth, beauty, and virility. The heroic death in combat is essentially, in the system of Homeric values, a "beautiful death."

At the moment when Hektor fell beneath the blows of Achilles, the poet makes it clear: "The Achaeans admired the commanding presence and the enviable beauty of Hektor,"[2] and Priam himself recalled, in comparing the death of an old man with that of a young hero: "In a young warrior killed by the enemy, torn apart by the sharp-pointed bronze, everything is handsome. Everything that he shows, though he is dead, is beautiful."[3] "Everything is beautiful," *panta kala*. The painter, in his way, translates on this vase this same ideology of the heroic body, laid bare under the bed of Achilles.

The attention given to the athletic body (fig. 53 to 61), in the context of gymnastic exercises is here replaced in the mythic scheme by the representation of these unusual deaths. One of the most remarkable and oldest examples is seen on the François vase. Kleitias twice represented Ajax carrying the corpse of Achilles; while Ajax is armed, the body of Achilles is naked, completely stripped. But this body is not bruised or repugnant: his long hair hangs down in uniform locks. All that he lets us see, though dead, is beautiful.

On a fragmentary cup attributed to Douris, one finds again the same motif: an armed warrior carries the unarmed body of his companion. The group is seen in three-quarter view and this change of angle allows a more elaborate representation of the anatomy and the face. The

3. *Iliad,* XXII, 71-73.

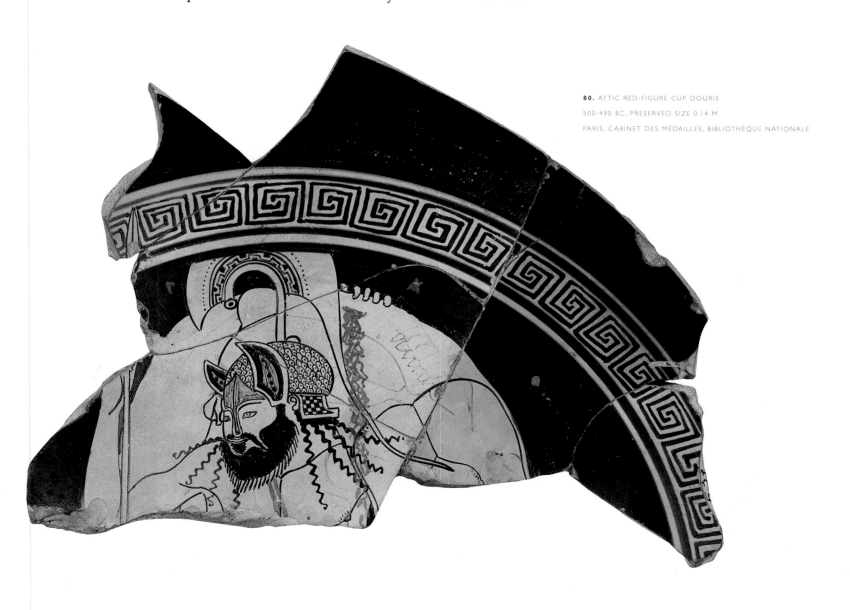

80. ATTIC RED-FIGURE CUP, DOURIS
500-490 BC, PRESERVED SIZE 0.14 M
PARIS, CABINET DES MÉDAILLES, BIBLIOTHÈQUE NATIONALE

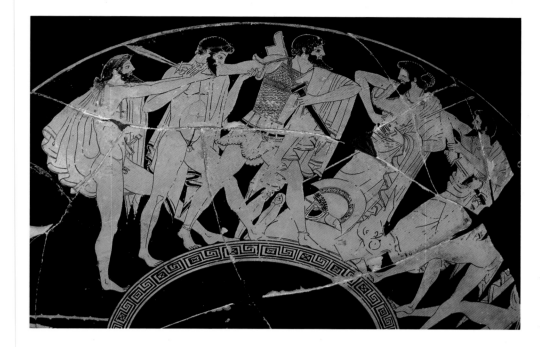

81, 82. ATTIC RED-FIGURE CUP, SIGNED DOURIS
490 BC, DIAMETER 0.34 M
VIENNA, KUNSTHISTORISCHES MUSEUM

bearer, without doubt Ajax, wears an especially finely-wrought helmet: high crest, skullcap of scales, nape-guard decorated in a checked pattern; the raised cheek-guards give the impression that this bearded face is endowed with menacing horns. Long locks of hair, hanging from beneath the helmet, spread out over the shoulders of the hero.

Leaning on his lance, whose point extends beyond the border of the image, he raises the body of his companion, which is displayed in a circular arc around his shoulders, legs to the left, head to the right. Of the face there remains on this fragment only the tip of the beard raised in the air. The stretched abdomen bleeds heavily, next to the mane of the bearer of whose right hand we see the fingertips. The red blood begins to mix with the locks of hair. The genitals of Achilles are visible level with the eyes of Ajax. Such a melange of living and dead, the confusion of high and low, the contrast between the ornamental richness of finely worked armor and the massive power of a bare and lifeless body, gives to this image, though it is fragmentary, a singular power of fascination. Only two letters remain: an "S" and a "K", remnants of the never-ending formula *ho pais kalos,* "the young man is handsome," which here echoes the heroic beauty of the dead Achilles.

One knows the importance of Achilles' armor in the *Iliad.* Homer describes at great length the shield which Hephaistos forged at the command of Thetis, in order to replace the weapons lent to Patroklos and taken by Hektor. After the death of Achilles, a dispute broke out between Odysseus and Ajax, each of whom laid claim to the arms of Achilles. One sees these weapons on a cup signed by Douris. The arms

83. REVERSE OF THE CUP, FIGURE 82

are lying on the ground, shield flat and helmet on top of it, as we have seen in the departure scene, here framed by two greaves and a rigid breastplate. To the left, a warrior in a breastplate with undone shoulder-guards lunges forward with a scabbard in his hand, sword drawn; two of his companions seize his arms to prevent him from striking. In the center, a man in a cloak with a spear in his hand intervenes, while at the right, symmetrically, a man draws his sword, held back by two companions. The Greeks try to separate Odysseus and Ajax.

One has here a rare scene of conflict among the Greeks themselves, a *stasis* which will be settled, as we see on the other side of the vase, by a vote. Athena, in the center, stands behind a sort of podium where the Greeks come to set down their tokens in turn. She holds her arms towards the victor on the left, Odysseus, who raises his hands to the sky, thrilled with the result; while to the right (the vase is fragmentary), Ajax turns, greatly vexed, hand on this forehead, head veiled. This repudiation by the Greeks would send him into a furious madness, and then to suicide. But the painter is here content to show the vote and the collective decision. This iconographic choice is not unimportant; it seems that during the time of this cup (around 490-480 BC), there was a more democratic version of the mythic episode. On vases of the 5th century BC, there exists practically no political scene showing civic activity – assembly, debate or voting. Here, the procedure used to put an end to the *stasis,* that of the vote, is therefore more remarkable. In this epic context, one meets a sort of politicization of the heroic community; but the procedure of the vote, which assures no secrecy since one comes to set down his token in front of everyone, is not necessarily that of the democracy of the 5th century BC, contemporary with the vase. The image shapes the meaning of epic through the categories of democracy.

The medallion of this same cup extends the evocation of this debate over the arms of Achilles. One sees on it two characters in a *vis-à-vis,* one bearded, the other beardless, handing down a set of armor. The manner in which the elements of armor are arranged is particularly noteworthy: cnemids upright on the ground, the breastplate in the center of the image, and the helmet at eye level. One has the impression of seeing the absent body of Achilles, whose armor alone suggests the silhouette. Dead and invisible, the hero is seemingly present in the cavity of his empty armor. The large notched shield bears in *episeme* a motif in silhouette: a lion devouring a doe, an animal metaphor for the savage power of the hero.

One reads around the medallion the signature of the painter, Douris. The figures are not named. Without doubt what we have here is Odysseus, bearded, receiving the arms of Achilles after the vote, or rather (even if the gestures do not seem to point in this direction) Odysseus giving the young Neoptolemos the arms of his father.

What is certain in any case is the symbolic prestige of these weapons, whose handing down is eagerly desired, as is the effect on one's appearance produced by the full panoply of this armor of Achilles. One finds here in a way the counterpart to what is shown in the fragment where Ajax carries the body of Achilles. A bare body or empty armor: Achilles as pictured is truly a hero, in both body and armor.

The painters, as is seen, were more interested in heroes and their armor than in war and tumultuous battles. It is however a theme which holds their attention because it allows one, in the mythic scheme, to express all the tragic violence of war: the motif of the destruction of Troy, the *Ilioupersis,* which marks the end of the kingdom of Priam and the disappearance of all his people.

One finds a particularly rich and complex version of this on a hydria attributed to the Kleophrades painter. The image forms a continuous frieze which unfolds on the shoulder of the vase and is composed of five

84. INTERIOR OF THE CUP, FIGURE 82

contiguous groups corresponding to five episodes in the Trojan cycle.

In the center near the palm tree of Apollo, old Priam is seated, in the manner of a supplicant, upon an altar; he holds his head in his two hands while the child Astyanax is stretched, body broken, on his knees. Priam is wounded on his head and shoulder; the child is also bloodstained, as well as the altar upon which they take refuge. Neoptolemos, the son of Achilles, has seized Priam by the shoulder and prepares to finish him off with a blow from his sharp *machaira*. This weapon is noteworthy because it is not the usual sword of hoplites; the dissymetrical blade characterizes the instrument as one which is used in sacrifice. Now, Priam is seated on the altar of Apollo to put himself under his protection. One sees the extent of the sacrilege: not only does Neoptolemus kill an old man and a child, but he does so in a temple with a sacrificial weapon, with no respect for the gods Priam invokes. One is far from the heroic battle; everything topples in the horror and the tragic violence.

The same happens with the group which appears to the left of the altar. The statue of Athena stands immobile. The goddess has the posture of a combatant, close to that which we have seen on the panathenaic amphoras, in a stiff and archaic style which makes her a statue to be venerated. A woman takes refuge at the foot of the statue, which she embraces, while turning all around with arm extended, to implore her assailant. Here we have Cassandra, the prophetess, whom Ajax prepares to rape. This dimension of desire and eroticism is made explicit by the way in which Cassandra's dress has slipped back from her shoulders, revealing her completely naked, body displayed, while the other women, huddled and wrapped up, are seated at the foot of the altar and the statue. Ajax, numb to pity, has already placed his hand on the nape of Cassandra's neck, and while Athena threatens him with her lance, he points his sword towards the body of his victim.

At the extreme left, Aeneas, preceded by his young son Ascanius, carries on his back the old Anchises, his father: three generations flee the city. To the right, on the other hand, Acamas and Demophon come to free the old Aethra, seated on the ground, mother of Theseus who was held hostage by the Trojans. Finally a Trojan woman, perhaps Andromache, tries to finish off with an enormous pestle a Greek who has placed his knee on the ground. Women, old men, children, all those we have seen in the scenes of leave-taking and the donning of armor representing the household, the *oikos,* for the defense of which the warrior leaves for combat, all these are here massacred, and raped,

and reduced to fighting with the energy of despair. The Greeks no longer respect the gods; their limitless violence is only imaginable – and able to be shown – on the level of myth and epic.

Parallel to these episodes of violence where one sees the ransacking of the city, of the *oikos,* and the ruin of the ties of kinship which constitute them, the painters have also represented an unimaginable form of war, that conducted by a group of women, the Amazons.

The examples of combat between Greeks and Amazons are quite numerous in Attic imagery from the 6th century BC. Sometimes they confront Herakles, who must seize the belt of their queen (this belt, for a Greek, is a symbol of marriage, which the Amazons did not want at any price); sometimes they come to the help of the Trojans, and Achilles, at the moment of finishing off their queen, Penthesilea, falls in love with her; and finally sometimes they invade Attica and are pushed back by Theseus, the mythical king of Athens, who carries off their queen Antiope. In all these cases, this race of women who are without men confronts the unmarried heroes who come very close to an impossible marriage. It is truly the family and procreation which are once again at play in these stories, but through a reversal unthinkable for a Greek: if a woman becomes a warrior, she "plays the man" in a way and can no longer be mother and wife. Such is the fate of the Amazons.

On a *pelike* from the end of the 5th century BC, a tree in the middle of the image defines the open space of the battlefield. An Amazon on a horse confronts two young Greek warriors. She is dressed in a checkered costume, typical of the oriental and barbarian world. With her lance she threatens a young naked man in a helmet who protects himself behind a large star-studded shield, while his companion, in a chlamys, his *petasos* fallen back on the nape of his neck like the horsemen seen parading past on the vase in the Louvre, comes to his assistance. The appearance of the young Greeks does not allow us to precisely identify the episode represented. It is certainly not Herakles; Theseus, accompanied by a young ephebe, would seem more likely. One is brought back to the motif which also figures on the metopes of the Parthenon: the city of Athens triumphant over oriental barbarism. The ideology of the city returns the women to their impossible otherness. In this city which one could define as a "men's club," a heroic figure such as the citizen-soldier could only be masculine.

◄ **87.** ATTIC RED-FIGURE PELIKE
MAY BE COMPARED WITH THE PAINTER OF LOUVRE G 433
400 BC, HEIGHT 0.37 M
WARSAW, NATIONAL MUSEUM

PASSAGES 5

In 1909, the folklore scholar Arnold van Gennep demonstrated, in a seminal study, the idea of the "rite of passage." He managed to show how certain practices sought to symbolically transform the status of an individual in a society, in making him pass from one state to another; for example from adolescent to adult through the rites of initiation, from young woman to wife or young man to husband, in marriage, or just as well through funerals, from the world of the living to that of the dead.

Each of these rites, which know many variations according to cultures and epochs, consists of the same phases according to van Gennep: a time of separation, then a time of waiting or latency, followed by a time of aggregation or integration.

Such a model, which permits the interpretation and comparison of a good number of ritual phenomena, even if it requires great nuance, could easily be applied to the ancient Greek world. In the case of funerals as well as that of marriage, one notices a passage and a transformation of individual status. But there is more, and this aspect will retain us here: in both cases the vases themselves are more than just a material support for the image. Not only is their iconography in keeping with the ceremony concerned, but the object itself has its own ritual function.

The principal cemetery in Athens, placed outside the double northwest gate, the Dipylon, is found near the potters' quarter and today bears the name Kerameikos. The connection between pottery and funerals is a very close one. The memorial vase is an integral part of the tomb in the case of the richest burials. The body is accompanied by vases which serve as offerings at the moment of burial. The location of the tomb is signaled in two ways: by an erected stone which in the classical era bore the name of the deceased and sometimes his sculpted image, and by a memorial krater whose foot was rooted in the sepulcher and whose basin served to offer libations to the dead. The krater which for the living makes possible the mixing of wine and assures the conviviality of the symposium, allows on the tomb the guarantee of a kind of symbolic continuity between the living and the dead.

The role of the vase as ritual element is fundamental in the case of funerals and one cannot be surprised to note that in the history of Greek art the production of funeral vases marks the starting point for the representation of the human figure. During the 8th century BC, in the era of the geometric style, when one sees the first figurative images appear, one encounters at first horses, birds, and human figures. As soon as the image became more complex, it dealt with processions of warriors, battles, and funeral scenes, the majority of which were found on large kraters, themselves placed upon the tomb of the deceased, as a marker designating the place for the devotion of the living.

One knows many vases of this type which, through their stylistic variations, present a remarkable unity. An example which is today in New York gives us a clear idea of this. The vase, of monumental size, is entirely covered with geometric motifs alternating with three figurative zones. The two lower zones are populated by a parade of chariots driven by warriors who move from left to right. The principal zone is found on the upper register, between the vertical handles. It represents the display of the body of the dead person *(prothesis)* mourned by his people. The space is organized according to tiered rows which display the elements of the image in a hierarchy. The body is laid out with the head to the right, placed on a bed whose pillar-like feet support a sort of canopy, represented by a checkerboard which fills the entire upper space of the image. The head of the deceased rests on a support marked by small triangles. No anatomical detail is indicated apart from the eye which occupies the entire face and a sort of long braid, which one also finds on the chariot drivers, and which one might think refers to the plumes of the helmets. The dead person must therefore have been a warrior. Near his head stands a small figure who with one hand touches his own head, and with the other the face of the deceased. At the foot of the bed another figure extends his arms towards the exposed corpse.

Below the bed six figures are seated, hands on their heads, in an attitude of lamentation. These are mourners whose feminine gender is indicated by the small lines in the armpits, the conventional sign in geometric art to mark the breasts. To the left of the bed a series of eleven mourners, standing this time, repeats the same gesture of lamentation. The repetitive multiplicity of these figures suggests the intensity of grief and the importance of the deceased. The right side of the scene is more original: one sees a row of warriors, wearing the same headgear as the deceased, swords at their sides. Almost all hold strings of dead animals which are not easy to identify: the last two carry birds, the two before them fish, the first two small quadrupeds without horns; the man at the head of the cortege perhaps holds shellfish. The eighth warrior, at the far right of the row, holds nothing and the straight-necked birds in front of him are certainly alive. This

last person is strange: he has a two-headed torso, four arms and four legs; one sees it as Siamese twins, the interpretation of which is not easy. It has often been proposed to see here the twins, sons of Poseidon and adversaries of Nestor, the Moliones to whom the *Iliad* alludes. But since this is a mythical figure, one is surprised to find it in four instances on this vase: in this scene, but also on the reverse, and twice in the parade of chariots on the lower register. Perhaps what we have here is the painter's attempt to represent two warriors side by side; he does the same in representing the harnessed horses, which have one body but two heads and eight feet. In this case the image would not deal with the myth of the Moliones, but on the contrary the myth would derive from the work of the painters. The myth would not produce the images, it is the image which would engender the stories which are echoed by Homer.

Regardless of what this double figure might be, the entire scene is noteworthy. Around the exposed body the women to the left mourn the deceased and the men to the right bring offerings. The image does not allow us to say more; but this food could be understood as intended for the dead himself or for the funeral banquet in his honor.

In the series of ritual acts which constitute the funeral, the painter's choice is significant. He depicts the moment when the deceased is displayed in his home, in the place where he lived, mourned by his people and acclaimed by his companions in arms. This visual experience, which for the last time places the dead under the gaze of the living, is fixed by the image on the vase, and then permanently placed on the tomb of the dead. The monument commemorates, in the space of the cemetery, the final instant spent by the dead person among his own. Of the three moments of passage – the display of the deceased in his home *(prothesis),* the transport to the cemetery *(ekphora),* and the final burial – the krater condenses the first and the last moments on one single object which fixes forever the honors given to the dead.

The decorated vase in this way does not content itself with reproducing the ritual in which it takes place: it gives it a model image which through its geometric rigor and its intensity aims to record the funerary practice.

The Greeks did not fail to invent new rituals and to open their minds to religious novelties, all the more easily since they lived within a religion which was not based on revelation, and which was not

90. ATTIC BLACK-FIGURE PLAQUE, BURGON GROUP
560-50 BC, LENGTH 0.44 M
PARIS, LOUVRE

dogmatic. But the funeral practices, because they assure familial continuity and allow one to manage throughout time the duration of the relationships between the living and the dead, seem particularly stable and conservative. The iconography of funeral rituals such as one observes in the geometric period of the 8th century BC remains practically unchanged up to the end of the classical period, and one can speak in this case of ritual conservatism.

The place accorded to the treatment of the corpse, to the greeting addressed by those living to the dead body before it finally passes to the invisible side, explains the need in the epic to recover the body of the hero killed in combat. Ajax, on the François vase, brings the corpse of Achilles far from the battlefield in order that it may receive the honors which are due (fig. 9). We have seen how Achilles himself took out his anger against the Trojans and avenged Patroklos by humiliating the mortal remains of Hektor. But in refusing to return this corpse to its people, in aggravating the grief of Priam, in preventing all funeral ritual, Achilles offends the gods: even the "best of the Achaeans" is not permitted to refuse burial to a deceased or to prevent his people from mourning him with dignity.

The importance of the time of display, the *prothesis,* in the funeral ritual is confirmed by numerous archaic and classical objects, in particular the funeral plaques intended to decorate the tombs. One of

the oldest of these is found today in the Louvre. It is an oblong plaque
provided with holes designed to attach it with pegs to the monument
itself. In the center, the deceased is laid out on a bed, his body entirely
covered by a blanket; only his head, resting on a cushion, is visible.
His eyes are closed, which is indicated by the very precise drawing of
the eyelashes. On each side of the face two women lean symmetrically, framing the deceased. Around the bed other women are
grouped, gesticulating and crying. To the left, a series of five bearded
men raise their right arms to salute the deceased. To the right, a man
and a woman hold out their arms towards the bed; behind them stands
a tree from which hang wreaths, offerings to the dead. Apart from the
bed, nothing denotes the domestic space, and the tree seems to
indicate an outdoor place, perhaps the courtyard of the house. The
image does not seek to describe the ritual place in detail but rather to
organize the relationship of gazes between the living and the dead.
Closest to the corpse are the women, while the men stand at more of a
distance. The hanging wreaths correspond more to the offerings which
one leaves at the tomb upon repeated visits than to the ritual elements
of *prothesis* such as we know from other sources, on the whole of the
series. This funeral plaque, attached to the tomb, seems to evoke by
anticipation the crowns offered during visits paid regularly by the
family of the deceased.

The same organization around the death bed is taken up again on a tall funeral amphora attributed to the Kleophrades painter. This type of oblong vase (which is not very functional) corresponds to an archaic form of amphora which is used only for ritual, just like the typology of the image. This vase, called a loutrophoros amphora, was intended to hold the water which is used to wash the deceased. It was then set down upon the tomb as a marker, just as the geometric kraters. On the belly one finds the ancient scheme: a bed upon which the deceased is displayed, his head raised up on a cushion, the chin held by a strap which prevents any deformity of the face. Around the bed many women pull their hair, in a gesture equivalent to that of the geometric figures, but one which the precision of the drawing makes more explicit. On the other side of the vase, a series of men come to salute the deceased while on the neck a pair of women approach, one of whom laments while the other carries a loutrophoros amphora exactly like the one which is used to show these scenes. On the lower register, and on a smaller scale, a frieze of horsemen seems to salute the deceased: one recognizes the geometric motif of the warriors as an indication of the social status of the dead man. One will notice here that the frieze is in black-figure while the vase is in red-figure. The use of the archaic technique for this frieze is yet another indication of the conservatism of this ritual vase.

Alongside the vases or plaques which mark the tomb, the painters also produced other series specifically intended to be left as offerings in or on the tomb. One such type of vase has always existed, but from the middle of the 5th century BC one sees the development of a particular series of objects reserved exclusively for this use. These are the white ground lekythoi, small vases for perfumed oil whose surface, covered with white slip, is painted with figures in outline which are often embellished in flat paints. The vases are very often decorated with funeral scenes.

A lekythos of this type shows its proper usage; the scene presents a tall stele erected on four steps. It is decorated with narrow strips of red cloth. Its rounded summit encroaches upon the decorative border of the vase to touch the ornamental palmette on the shoulder. To the right, a woman whose dress is partially worn away carries a large flat basket containing two lekythoi, two wreaths and various black and red strips of cloth. To the left, a young man in a black cloak holds a strip of cloth out towards the tomb. In this scene the stele is at the center of the ritual of offerings

92. ATTIC WHITE-GROUND LEKYTHOS, NOT ATTRIBUTED

470-60 BC, HEIGHT 0.39 M

PARIS, LOUVRE

and visitation. It constitutes the visible sign of the invisible deceased. Once buried in his place under the ground among the dead, the deceased is regularly honored by the living who keep his memory alive through the offerings. The stele, decorated with strips of cloth, and sometimes anointed with oil, is treated like a corpse. From the visual experience of the *prothesis,* the final look before the burial, follows the visit to the tomb; the stele serves then as the place of meeting and connection between the world of the living and that of the dead. In the picture, this same stele serves as the central axis of the visitation scenes.

On a lekythos in Athens, two women stand on each side of a tomb. The one on the right holds a flat basket containing fruits and wreaths. The one on the left holds out an offering while bringing her hand to her face as if to wipe away a tear or to indicate her quiet thought. In the background of the image two lekythoi are hanging in the air; the scene is situated outside, one cannot think that these objects are hung on a wall; these are only signs meant to increase the funerary value of the lekythos, at the same time the carrier of the ritual image and an offering at the tomb. The image, by this reflexive procedure, once again shows its proper usage.

The stele itself, topped with a pediment which is filled by a large palmette, bears a series of marks on five lines which bring to mind an inscription. But what we have here is the image of a text, because this inscription made of plain little sticks cannot be read. On the funeral monument the name of the deceased, carved in the stone, is perpetuated among the living who, in reading it, pronounce it aloud. Here the painter has left unspecified what is to be read, entrusting the buyer of the vase with the task of saying the name of the recipient of the offering. The image suggests a generic scene; it gives to the ritual a quasi-theoretical form, while the ritual practice strengthens the familial bonds, as well as the utterance of the names which form the framework of these rituals of commemoration in the particularity of the proper name.

The lekythos painters explored in a particularly subtle manner the visual possibilities which provide the imaging of the relationship between the world of the living and that of the dead, between the

93, 94. ATTIC WHITE-GROUND LEKYTHOS, INSCRIPTIONS PAINTER
450 BC, HEIGHT 0.36 M
ATHENS, ARCHAEOLOGICAL MUSEUM

visible and the invisible. Thus, on another lekythos, two visitors frame a stele: a young man at the left, leaning on his staff, makes a gesture indicating a conversation with the woman on the right who holds a helmet and a shield, as in the scenes of armament and departure of the warrior. Between these two visitors, is the stele upon whose steps is seated a warrior who holds two spears in his left hand. He is seen in three-quarter view, and his expression appears vacant, lost on a horizon which the two who are standing and speaking do not seem to see; this countenance, facing almost fully forward, meets no gaze other than that of the viewer. He is elsewhere, present in the image but outside the dialogue. This presence, in the center of the image, superimposed on the stele, functions as the visible sign of an absence. The figure seated on the steps is the image of the deceased, whose stele indicates the final resting place and of whom the visitors bring to mind the absence. The arms which are held by the woman at the right are not offerings, but the symbol of the relationship with the dead warrior whom she honors, which she would keep alive during her lifetime. The scene is not the description of the putting on of armor at the tomb. It evokes, at the tomb, a scene which one day took place in the *oikos,* their common dwelling. Time and space are displaced and confused in an image which intermingles past and present, visible and invisible, a scene which makes material all the symbolic ritual of the funeral offering, since it reestablishes in an image the bonds which unite the members of the same group, both present and absent, living and dead.

Toward the end of the 5th century BC, with a great economy of means, and through the elaboration of relatively simple iconographic schemes, the painters achieved the development of the symbolic efficacy of the funeral rituals, which they were not content to reproduce in a documentary style, but whose significance they visually prolonged.

The same happened, in various ways, with the rituals of marriage. Like funerals, but with obvious differences, marriage is a passage, a change of state, particularly for the young girl who, subject to her father, is then entrusted to her husband. In changing hands she changes houses. Greek marriage is a private act, an accord sealed by the father of the bride and the husband, an agreement whose validity depends on the publicity made of it. This is the purpose of the nuptial procession which accompanies the newlyweds from one house to the other, to the glimmer of torches and the sound of matrimonial songs.

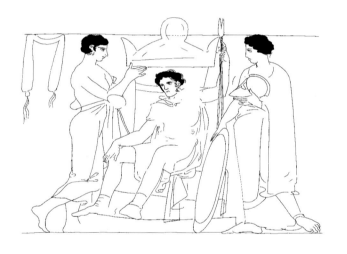

95, 96. ATTIC WHITE GROUND LEKYTHOS, GROUP R
410 BC, HEIGHT 0.48 M
ATHENS, ARCHAEOLOGICAL MUSEUM

Among the numerous episodes which make up weddings – the agreement with the father, the ritual bathing of the spouses, the presentation of gifts, the family meal, the unveiling of the bride, the wedding night, the awakening of the couple, etc. – the painters favored two moments and two particular points of view.

The first is that of the transfer of the bride from one house to the other. The procession moves by foot or by cart, often on a chariot which ennobles the scene, in returning to the mythic models of which the François vase presents for us a major example. On the Florence krater, as we have seen, the gods come in a procession to greet the newlyweds, Thetis and Peleus, now established in their home. Peleus receives them near the domestic altar where the alliance with the gods is made, while Thetis is seated in the palace. The half-open door flap allows the new wife, who raises the side of her veil, to appear. To guarantee the validity of the marriage, the bride must be seen, and the images make a show of this passage.

On a *pyxis* in the Louvre, one witnesses such a procession. The form of the vase itself serves in making visible this dynamic of passage. The *pyxis* is a box for jewels or perfume, an object of feminine use, for ornaments or finery. The pictorial surface is cylindrical, without any handle which could interrupt the continuity of the image, which unfolds in a circle around the vase. In order to comprehend the totality, one must turn the vase and follow the procession with one's eyes.

We leave the house, marked by a door. The couple advances towards the right: the young man has grasped his young bride by the wrist, in a gesture which could itself symbolize the marriage. The young bride is followed by a woman standing before the door who adjusts her clothes; she is thus surrounded by a play of hands which embodies the transition from the house which she leaves toward the one where she is led. The rest of the frieze shows Apollo, the god with

the laurel, next to his sister Artemis, the archer, the goddess who accompanies young girls to the threshold of marriage. The presence of the gods, made visible in the image, guarantees the prosperity of the marriage. Further away a pair of adults receives the procession; these are the parents of the groom who are receiving the newlyweds in their new home. The door which served as the point of departure is found again here, as the point of arrival of the procession. Because it is closed, one cannot decide if it designates the house which one leaves or the one which one joins; the double door thus presents itself as the simplest sign of passage, from door to door.

Once again one measures the economy of means with which the image accounts for everything that goes beyond simple description, since it integrates the gods in the ritual that is depicted, assuring in this way its symbolic efficacy.

The second aspect selected by the painters from the ensemble of acts which constitute the marriage ceremony is still more directly linked with the young wife, when she is seen among her female friends, in the process of preparing herself or of receiving gifts. Again, the typology of the vases is connected with the necessities of the ritual. Two shapes are almost exclusively tied to marriage. On one hand we have the loutrophoros amphora, already encountered for funerals, which contains the water for the nuptial bath and whose decoration takes up either the theme of the procession, or that of finery and gifts. On the other hand a type of krater mounted on a conical foot, the *lebes gamikos* – nuptial cauldron – is exclusively reserved for marriage and is among the gifts offered to the bride.

Such a vase appears placed upon the knees of a woman seated at the center of the scene on a krater in the Louvre, surrounded by other women who present her with the wedding gifts. A second vase of the same type is carried by the woman on the right, along with a box and some fabric. To the left, behind the chair of the bride, another companion holds a wickerwork box. In the background is suspended a *saccos,* the cap which serves to hold the hair.

The support of this vase is also decorated with analogous feminine figures. One holds a fabric hair-band, and the other a wickerwork box. Between them a flared basket stands on the floor: it is the *calathos,* the basket for wool, characteristic of the domestic activity of women. The multiplication of vases, boxes and contents offered here as gifts to the wife serves to indicate in a concrete way the domestic wealth which constitutes the dowry. But also, in a more metaphorical manner, to indicate a form of confinement linked to the arrangement and accumulation of goods. The woman, in turn, is sometimes thought of as a container, a jar or a vase, which mythology echoes with the jar (and not the box) of Pandora, or with the coffer of Danae.

Many of these nuptial images are constructed around the same model: the bride, seated at the center, is the focus of all the attention and the interaction is built around her, whether she is receiving gifts, or whether she is preparing for marriage by making herself beautiful. Mirrors, perfumes and wreaths are brought in to produce this seductive beauty, this source of desire without which marriage is not fruitful.

On an oblong perfume vase, a red-figure alabastron, one experiences the totality of these values. The young wife is seated before her wool basket; she holds a wreath, while above her, in the background, is suspended a veil decorated with crosses the same as her chiton. Behind her a small servant holds an alabastron similar to the support vase. Feminine beauty, the preparations of which are like an entertainment, finds its admirer within that same image. On the other side of the vase stands a young man, leaning on his staff, holding out a belt to his young wife. This belt is not a simple ornament of dress; it is the very emblem of marriage. In untying it, the young husband seals the union of the couple. Between these two figures a double inscription comes to complete the scene. Near the young man one reads: *Timodemos kalos,* "Timodemos is handsome," according to the familiar formula. Above the wool basket, the feminine adjective qualifies the woman *he nymphe kale,* "the bride is beautiful." *Nymphe* is a generic

100. FULL VIEW OF AN ALABASTRON, FIGURES 101, 102

▶ **101, 102.** ATTIC RED-FIGURE ALABASTRON, NOT ATTRIBUTED

470 BC, HEIGHT 0.17 M

PARIS, CABINET DES MÉDAILLES, BIBLIOTHÈQUE NATIONALE

term, which does not designate the woman in her singular identity, but rather the bride in general. The word *nymphe* applies as much to the young girl before her marriage as it does to the married woman before the birth of her first child. On this perfume vase, belt and wreath show, in the exchange, the bonds which unite the couple, given to us to see as a model of beauty: *kalos* and *kale.*

The François vase provides, as we have seen, a paradigm of marriage in showing the visit which the gods make to Thetis and Peleus (fig. 5). Other mythical scenes permit the understanding of other aspects of marriage. A small amphora in the Louvre shows a rare and surprising scene. One sees on it a procession reduced to its most simple expression: on a chariot appears a couple, and near the harness is a musician. But the inscriptions specify the name of the singer: Apollo, the musician *par excellence,* the god of the cithara with the ivory frame, as well as the names of the spouses: Cadmos and Harmonia. Harmonia is the daughter of Ares and Aphrodite; she embodies the accord between violence and war, which are the domain of Ares, and feminine seduction, the domain of Aphrodite. In marrying Cadmos, she is with him at the origins of Thebes. The music which accompanies the married couple, the song of Apollo, makes this harmony which presides over the marriage sonorous. But there is more: the team pulling the chariot is not an ordinary one; it is composed of a lion and a boar, wild animals, more often hunted than trained. No text allows us to clarify the reasons for such an equipage, but one can compare this image with a story told by Apollodoros: "Apollo served Admetos, the king of Pherae (in Thessaly) at the moment when Admetos sought Alcestis, daughter of Pelias, in marriage. Pelias proclaimed that he would grant his daughter to whomever could harness a lion and a boar together to a chariot. Apollo did this and brought the team to Admetos."[1]

Apollo succeeded in doing the impossible: he tamed two wild animals and put them side by side under the yoke, permitting the marriage of his patron. The Louvre amphora shows us nothing of Admetos; but Apollo is there, guarantor of another marriage. The figures of harness and yoke function as a metaphor for marriage, an alliance which demands harmony and domestication. The presence of the god of music is not accidental; he is here in his proper place to accompany these mythic weddings which reveal in a metaphoric way mastery over the tension between violence and harmony.

◄ **103.** ATTIC BLACK-FIGURE AMPHORA, DIOSPHOS PAINTER
500 BC. HEIGHT 0.21 M
PARIS, LOUVRE

1. Apollodoros, *Library,* I, 9, 15.

MEN AND GODS 6

The major act which, apart from prayers and offerings, gives form to the relationship between men and gods in the ancient Greek world is the act of sacrifice, *thusia,* in which an animal is put to death and then partially consumed in the course of a collective meal, or, in the case of a sacrifice to the infernal gods, entirely burned in their honor (holocaust), without being eaten. The choice of an animal victim, more precisely of a domestic animal (sheep, cow, or pig), through the familiarity which it implies between man and his victim, gives to the sacrifice a violent and quasi-murderous dimension that was often problematic for the Greeks.

A good many mythical stories try to account for this sacrificial practice; whether it be that of Prometheus, the first one to arrange the sharing of meat between men and gods, or that of Sopatros, who came to Athens to cleanse the bloodstain brought about by the death of the first sacrificed ox.

The image in turn treats this practice in its own way, not simply by reproducing the sacrificial ritual in its different stages, but in elaborating on it, starting from the specific act, of which the representations function as models.

If one confines oneself, at first, to a linear description of the sacrifice in its temporal development, one can distinguish successively the procession – *pompe* – which leads the victim towards the temple, and the sacrifice itself, which takes place at the altar. Once put to death, the animal is cut up and then the parts of meat are first boiled and then put on a spit and roasted on the fire of the sacrificial altar. A meal follows, where the group who made the sacrifice shares this food, almost always in the setting of a feast in honor of one god or another.

The sacrificial images which we know belong essentially to two distinct categories, reliefs and vases. The reliefs have a very particular function: they are themselves offerings, placed in the temples by the faithful. They are hung on walls or fixed on pillars, often accompanied by an inscription which specifies the identity of the god to whom it is being dedicated. The reliefs are fixed, always seen in the same context: the space of the sanctuary, with for onlookers the faithful who have come to pray or to sacrifice in their turn in this place. Here we are dealing with a reflexive image, and the majority of these reliefs follow the same iconographic model. On one hand, they represent, around an altar, the procession which approaches, and on the other hand, on a larger scale, the god or gods for whom the sacrifice is intended.

The scheme used by the sculptors is invariable. Often the frame of the relief itself, which resembles a portico, evokes the place in which the sacrifice occurs, as well as the place where this relief is displayed, the place where spectators come to pray to these votive images.

In terms of the vases, we shall see that the iconographic schemes are more varied; the vase itself is a moveable object, used in particular at the symposium, which often followed a meal of meats coming from the sacrifice. And so the context of use permits a greater choice of composition and a greater variety in its plasticity and in its themes. We know nearly 250 votive reliefs from the classic era which represent a sacrificial procession; but there exist more than 430 vases relating to this ritual, and this important series contains all sorts of variations, as much in terms of the moment during the sacrifice that is chosen as in the very kind of sacrifice represented, which often refers to a particular mythical story.

We cannot give here an account of all the riches in this group; we must limit ourselves to several characteristic examples.

Let us begin with a krater in Vienna, dating from around 420 BC. The vase itself, with its large mouth, serves to mix the wine and the water which the drinkers will consume. Near the lip, a frieze of laurel, in a large ornamental band, crowns the vase; this is a commonplace motif, but one which, combined here with a sacrificial image, recovers all its festive value.

The principal scene corresponds to the moment when the procession arrives near the altar. The scheme is entirely classical, with very little difference in detail; only some very small inscriptions painted in a contrasting white indicate the figures by name and bring the representation up to the level of myth. Here we have Herakles making a sacrifice on the isle of Lemnos to the goddess Chryse.

The son of Zeus stands upright at the center of the composition. Dressed in a cloak cinched at the waist, crowned with leaves, he in no way resembles the hero in the lion skin: with neither bow nor club, unarmed, he is identified only by the inscription which accompanies him. Having become the sacrificer, Herakles assumes the bearing and the gestures of the ritual: his right hand raised, he greets the victim, adorned with strips of cloth on the horns. The animal is led by the faithful companion of the hero, the young Iolaos, who is dressed as a hunter, as if to remind us that, even though Herakles is unarmed, which the ritual requires, the hunt with dogs and the mastery of the savage world are not far away.

The left hand of Herakles is open, in a gesture of prayer turned

104. ATTIC RED-FIGURE KRATER
IMITATION OF THE CADMOS PAINTER
420 BC, HEIGHT 0.30 M
VIENNA KUNSTHISTORISCHES MUSEUM

towards the altar where the flame of sacrifice burns. Here again, we observe the subtle discrepancies (which the comparison with the following images will make more evident) between the "standard" sacrifice and this heroic sacrifice. The altar is not formed by an architectural block of squared-off and tidily arranged rocks topped by a table decorated with spirals, but by a mass of large boulders, themselves heaped upon a rock which is indicated by simple white lines in the arc of a circle, upon which lies a larger boulder that serves as its center. The general impression is that of a rustic altar in a rocky place, confirmed by a minimal indication of landscape to the right, near the handle.

At the back of the altar on a simple low column is found a small statue of the archaic type: standing, legs close together, the rigid body wearing a tight embroidered dress cinched at the waist, she is presented full-face, arms outstretched and hands raised, captured in a pose symmetrical to the gesture of prayer of Herakles. This female divinity with her face turned towards the viewer of the image receives with her gesture the offering which is being prepared. Erected in this way near the altar, the statue forms with the boulder the axis of the image and clearly marks the receiver of the sacrifice: the local goddess Chryse.

To the right of the altar, other actors are present. A young anonymous man is leaning towards a small box of which he removes the cover; this accessory, frequently represented on reliefs and more rarely on vases, contains without doubt some of the ritual objects.

Near the altar stands a feminine figure with wings spread, which an inscription names Nike. Often translated as Victory, the term personifies the idea of success and successful outcome; it is not necessarily a military or athletic victory; here her presence marks the acceptance by the divinity of an offering which must be favorable for the hero. This Nike holds in her hands two objects essential to the sacrificial rite: in her right hand a receptacle, without doubt metal, the *chernips,* which contains the water with which the victim will be sprinkled by the sacrificer; in the left hand a tray decorated with three branches (most often it is a three-pointed basket), the *kanoûn,* upon which are placed the grains which will be thrown into the fire, and the sacrificial knife for putting the animal to death.

The image does not show the knife, and does not allow the appearance of any of the violence which is implicit in the sacrifice. On the contrary, it seeks to put in order, in a solemn and peaceful manner, the relationships between men and animals, and between men and gods. While bringing together the extremely precise and "realistic" details of the sacrificial ritual, in particular the technical objects which make it possible – altar, statue, basin, basket, crowns, and strips of cloth – the image makes visible the presence of Nike as an actor in the ritual, instead of a simple human assistant. The image is not content to describe the ritual, but manifests the effectiveness of it through the active presence of divine figures.

The goddess Chryse is here present as an image, in the form of a statue whose archaic aspect guarantees great age, which is a venerable characteristic. Nike herself is a "real" and effective presence, on the same plane as the heroes and the humans assembled around the altar.

In the sacrificial order proposed to the drinkers on a banquet vase, the decoration makes visible and close the symbolic effectiveness of the sacrifice. The presence of Nike is not linked with the fact that what we have here is Herakles and a mythical sacrifice; one sees her on other vases, in non-mythological contexts where she marks with her presence the divine aspect active in the ritual.

The vase painters, as opposed to the sculptors of reliefs, were not limited to the representation of the procession towards the altar. They were interested in other stages, which are never "snapshots," but images which combine various gestures and various objects to bring into view in a synthetic form that which is pertinent in the ritual. This was already the case in the preceding image, where a flame appears on the altar even though the victim is not yet slaughtered. The fire which burns evokes the sacrificial activity and the portion reserved for the gods, without which one would be obliged to believe that it is lit upon the arrival of the procession to the altar.

▶▶ **105.** DETAIL OF KRATER, FIGURE 104

The medallion of a cup in the Louvre attributed to the Epidromos painter is exceptional from the point of view of the choice of the moment, because the sacrificial knife *(machaira)* usually hidden in the basket of grains is here held up in the air in a very explicit manner by a bearded sacrificer who is standing before an altar. The scene takes place outside, as is indicated by the palm tree standing at the left, perhaps in reference to Artemis or Apollo, of whom it is sometimes the sacred tree. A young beardless assistant is squatting near the altar with a piglet in his arms. He supports with his left hand the snout of the animal, which he raises while holding its throat towards the altar. The man with the knife shows with his left hand the place where the blood of the victim must spurt at the moment of slaughter. The logic of

the choice is different here: the painter prefers the blood and the slaughter to the calm approach to the altar. Indeed, one observes on the altar itself large red strokes which indicate past sacrifices.

The blood constitutes the portion for the gods, along with the smoke from the fat and the burned bones. Lucian, in the 2nd century AD, when he wanted to be ironic about sacrificial practices and popular superstition, described the gods in this way, quoting Homer: "The immortals look towards the earth and turn their eyes in every direction while leaning over to see if some fire has been lit or if some smell of fat is rising on spirals of smoke. And when a sacrifice is made, they have a really good time; with mouths open they breathe in the smoke and suck up the blood spilled near the altars, as well as the flies." [1]

The Epidromos painter obviously does not share this critical point of view. In showing the slaughtering knife and the blood which stains the altar, he prefers – for once – the marks of killing and the image of this blood for which the gods are thirsty.

But the representation of such violence remains unusual and rare; it is generally connected with a mythical context, such as, for example, the case of the sacrifice of the young Polyxena, killed in honor of Patroklos, upon whose tomb the Greek warriors poured her blood.

The majority of the sacrificial images avoid the moment of violence in order to keep in mind, before or after the killing, other forms of contact between men and gods around the altar.

On a krater in the Louvre, similar to the one in Vienna and like it crowned at the lip with ornamental laurels, the sacrificial scene is constructed around an altar. Behind it, a laurel tree occupies a central place in the axis of the image. This altar, itself stained with blood, supports a series of regularly spaced planks of wood, seen from their ends and sides, in two layers. A fire is lit, indicated by the white markings. Above these flames, the meats are roasting on long iron spits *(obeloi),* held by a young assistant to the left of the scene. Near the altar a bearded priest wearing a crown holds in his hand an object which is difficult to identify, and about which opinions diverge. It is a round irregular mass taken out of the fire, which one interprets as a flour cake *(pelanos)* or as a part of the entrails *(splanchna),* which seems doubtful. To the right a young assistant who occupies a position analogous to that of Nike in the scene with Herakles holds a tray with three branches *(kanoûn)* and a wine jug *(oinochoe),* the contents of which he seems to pour on the altar. All the

◄ **106.** ATTIC RED-FIGURE CUP, EPIDROMOS PAINTER
500 BC. INTERIOR DIAMETER 0.19 M
PARIS, LOUVRE

1. Lucian, *On Sacrifices,* 9.

107. ATTIC RED-FIGURE KRATER, POTHOS PAINTER
420 BC. HEIGHT 0.33 M
PARIS, LOUVRE

▶ 108. DETAIL OF KRATER, FIGURE 107

gestures of these three actors are concentrated on the altar; above this highly symbolic object, the geometric place of the exchange between men and gods, are gathered all the elements which make up the sacrifice: blood, fire, meat, grains *(pelanos),* and wine for the libation.

One clearly sees here the extent to which the image is synthetic: it does not show the succession of gestures and their connection to each other, as would a documentary film; but joins them by putting next to each other all the pertinent objects which are necessary for the proper unfolding of the sacrifice.

But it does still more. To the right of the image there stands immobile, with one arm under his cloak and the other holding a long laurel branch, an apparently human figure which this laurel indicates as the god Apollo. Present at the sacrifice which is offered to him, the god is visible not in the form of a statue but in that of an anthropomorphic figure, totally integrated within the sacrifice, the acceptance of which he guarantees by his presence.

Through these three images a standard pattern for the sacrifice is constructed; this model puts in place gestures, spaces, instruments and symbolic elements in order to restore for the ancient viewer the essence of what is pertinent and proper to show.

In Attic imagery, the bond between gesture and ritual instrument is found again in a much more frequent manner on the occasion of libations. We are not dealing any more with a bloody sacrifice but with an offering of liquids, generally wine, in honor of the gods. Technically the libation consists of pouring a part of it on the altar, and then the rest is drunk by the one who makes the libation and those who are associated with him, his family, friends, and relatives. The word which designates the libation *(sponde)* signifies elsewhere in the plural *(spondai)* "the truce." It is therefore a form of sharing and making alliances in which both men and gods are involved, marking by this gesture the bond which unites them. The objects used to make a libation are basic: a jug which allows serving in a drinking cup or in a phiale, and a small cup without handles or foot; from this cup one pours their portion to the gods and then drinks in turn.

No ritual constraint predetermines in any strict manner the form which the libation must take: neither in space nor in time. One can pour on the ground or on a particular object: on a krater, or on an altar. The moment of libation is variable; it generally has to do with ritually marking the beginning or the end of an activity, waking up, departure, return, the start

of a banquet, etc. One has seen how the woman serves the wine of the libation which the warrior makes at the moment of going to war. The image frequently isolates this minimal gesture, without specifying the circumstances, as a simple mark of piety with respect to the gods.

In this same way, on a cup in the Louvre, the interior medallion highlights the very same type of ritual continuum. A young man wearing a wreath stands upright with arm extended, phiale in hand, in front of an altar upon which he makes a libation. The circle of the medallion partially conceals the altar of which one sees only the spiral edge; one will notice a small vegetable branch similar to the young man's crown lying on the altar, as well as patches of blood, a sign of the sacrificial activity that may occur at any time. Opposite the altar, a partially visible chair indicates without doubt that this is an interior domestic space rather than a sanctuary. But in fact, nothing is specified apart from the gesture of offering and the connection between men and gods which the altar implies. It is up to the drinker, in using the vase, to construct, if he wishes, a verbal commentary which would specify the moment, the place, and the recipient of a gesture which takes, from its commonplace nature, exemplary value.

The libation marks the bond between those who make it and the gods for whom it is intended. As an image, it acquires additional meaning and indicates the venerable nature of the gods, who sometimes take possession of the phiale, which then becomes the symbol of the offering which they receive.

We must now consider the gods and their representation. Greek art, as we know, generally gave them human form. The anthropomorphism of the Greek gods distinguishes them from other ancient pantheons, such as the Egyptian and the Near-Eastern, in which the hybrid forms and animal components are common. In the archaic and classical Greek world, the gods have human form, and frequently the imagery shows them closely related to humans. Sculpture has elaborated ideal figures in which the bodies of gods take on an appearance of perfection of which humanity is only a pale reflection. The same in the epic poems, when the gods indirectly reveal themselves to humans, in their epiphanies. Their body is always unchanging, young and beautiful; they know neither aging nor decrepitude, which are the fate of mortals. As J.P. Vernant has shown, the bodies of gods are super-bodies, made with brilliance, power, and beauty.

In ceramics, the gods are frequently represented; the painters

109. ATTIC RED-FIGURE CUP, MACRON
480 BC, MAXIMUM DIAMETER 0.36 M
PARIS, LOUVRE

delighted in showing their grandeur as well as their actions. Contrary to the monotheistic religions which make of their one god the creator of the world, the Greek gods are a part of the world; they act in it and experience adventures which the poets recount and the painters represent. The stories concerning the origin of the world show quite well how the primordial Chaos gave birth to the powers which in turn engendered the gods. Hesiod's *Theogony* is one of these poems which acquaints us with the successive genealogies of the gods, up to the establishment of Zeus as master of Olympus.

Many pictorial variations echo these traditions and represent the society of the gods, their loves and their conflicts. From this vast corpus, we will extract here several sufficiently diverse examples, not to reconstruct these traditions in their entirety, but to bring to mind some of their more striking aspects.

The first example is a unique image, for which the interpretation, since it has no parallels, is not certain. It is a cup attributed to the painter Douris, from around 480 BC. A woman sits on a slightly elevated throne holding a phiale in her right hand. On her head is a sort of tightly-worn scarf, a *saccos,* and the nape of her neck is covered by a part of her cloak, a bit in the manner of a bride. This appearance, and her seated position, give her a majestic air which is confirmed by the long scepter that she holds in her left hand. Nothing in her appearance would allow us to go any further in the identification of this royal figure, were she not identified by an inscription in front of her face: she is Hera, the wife of Zeus, master of Olympus.

Facing her, standing immobile with a scepter in hand, is a bearded man whom we would be able to understand as Zeus himself, if an inscription at his back did not come to shatter our illusion: this is Prometheus. What is more, the lack of symmetry between the two figures – feminine and masculine, seated and standing – reverses the usual roles of the enthroned man with the phiale and the woman serving him. Here the goddess reigns supreme and Prometheus does her homage. In her left hand she holds, along with her scepter, a floral ornament in the form of a highly stylized double palmette, which is generally not encountered in the main field of the image, but more often on the handles and on the marginal areas. In integrating at the heart of the image these non-mimetic elements, the painter adds beauty and brilliance to the figures, and this is one way to convey the divine dimension of these anthropomorphic presences.

The gesture of libation is central in this image. At the crossing of the two scepters, in the geometric center of the composition, the phiale which Hera holds is the sign of the bond which unites her to Prometheus. But what is the nature of this bond? Prometheus, as we remember, belonged to the generations of primordial times; he is the son of the Titan Iapetos, just as Hera and Zeus were descended from the Titan Cronos. According to another tradition, one which is doubtful, he was the son of Hera herself who was raped by the giant Eurymedon. On the medallion of this cup one will see the unique meeting of these Titans, born of disorder and chaos, here peaceful and orderly, ruled so to speak by the geometry of the throne and its pedestal, highlighted by the chiasmus which inscribes in the image the figure of the crossed scepters like the letter x (chi) of the Greek alphabet.

But this image awakens other echoes, if one looks at the exterior of the cup, whose two faces answer each other. One represents a *comos*, a procession of drinkers, of what one could say is the classic type, with a musician and dancers. On the other side, the procession is composed of satyrs and a maenad who accompany Dionysos and Hephaistos. The god of wine has taken the god of the smithy by the wrist. This gesture recalls that of the weddings such as we have seen on the pyxis in the Louvre (fig. 98); the preliminary sketch shows that the painter had at first simply placed these two gods side by side, and then modified the position of the arm of Dionysos grasping Hephaistos. Of course we are not dealing here with weddings; but the procession, which has the appearance of a *comos*, metaphorically evokes in the choice of gesture the passage and reintegration of Hephaistos into Olympus. We have seen (on the François vase, fig. 12, 13) the meaning in which this episode can be understood. The power of wine broke the resistance of Hephaistos, who agreed to come rescue his mother, Hera, from the throne in which she was trapped.

Therefore, it is the enthroned figure of Hera which we find on the medallion of this cup. The connection between these three surfaces is purely associative. The exterior scenes play upon the homologies between the world of men and the world of the gods, human *comasts* and mythical procession. On the inside, the wine of libation marks the coming together of the Olympians and a sort of peaceful accord, after the battles which set Zeus, master of the gods, against Prometheus, the rebel and thief of fire, whom we can place on the side of Hephaistos.

This medallion does not recount any particular episode, but brings

◀ 110. ATTIC RED-FIGURE CUP, DOURIS
480 BC, MAXIMUM DIAMETER 0.39 M
PARIS, CABINET DES MÉDAILLES, BIBLIOTHÈQUE NATIONALE

the mythical figures together and connects their fields of action: the Olympian sovereignty and the mastery over fire which, in turn, are evoked in a more narrative method on the exterior of the cup.

Not all the scenes between the gods are as enigmatic for us. One which figures on a hydria attributed to the Berlin painter belongs to a rich series in which one sees the divine twins, Artemis and Apollo. They are here reunited around an altar marked with blood upon which burns a high flame; although the ritual is not represented, these marks refer to the sacrifice of which the painter shows only the recipients. Apollo at the left holds in one hand a cithara, the string instrument of virtuosos, and in the other the phiale for libations. His sister Artemis holds the complementary vase, the *oenochoe,* which serves to fill the phiale. The two divinities who are thus isolated are not in the process of offering libations to themselves, as has often been thought. The gods do not lack offerings, and do not need to serve themselves; they hold in their hands the objects which serve to honor them and mark their venerable character.

Other assemblies of gods are more rich, more complex, and more unexpected, such as for example the one which decorates a small amphora in the Cabinet des Médailles. Four divinities are grouped around Zeus, who is seated at the center of the composition on a chair which is in the form of a cube. He holds a scepter and a thunderbolt – in the form of a double palmette – in his left hand. He turns towards his daughter Athena, who wears a helmet and is armed with a spear, and who salutes him by raising her left hand. She is followed by Hermes, who carries a caduceus. Facing Zeus and opposite Athena stands Hera, wearing a *polos* on her head and saluting with her right hand. Ares, in a helmet, is seated at the right of this scene.

No particular event seems to be evoked by this scene which joins together, in a game of salutes, gazes, and orientations, a specific group of divinities, a sort of pantheon in miniature. We are not dealing with an entire assembly of Olympians (as we have seen parading past at the wedding of Thetis and Peleus on the krater of Ergotimos), but simply with a choice within this ensemble. The image constructs, in accordance with the laws of Greek polytheism, a particular configuration which creates correlations and puts the relationships between the gods into a hierarchy: Zeus is in the center, between his acknowledged wife Hera and his divine daughter Athena. The two goddesses on either side of Zeus answer each other in their gestures. Ares forms the masculine counterpart of Athena. The image makes the connection between these two warrior divinities become visible: their spears meet above the head of Zeus. Finally Hermes at the left occupies here the position of a ferryman, as if he were introducing Athena into a face-to-face between Zeus and Ares.

The inscriptions which accompany each of these divine figures are not necessary for their identification; the caduceus, the armor, and the thunderbolt allow us to recognize Hermes, Athena, Ares and Zeus without any possible doubt. Only Hera could be confused with other goddesses (Demeter, for example). The name next to the figure therefore does not have a didactic role; it intensifies at the linguistic level the presence of the divinity, who is both painted and named. The names of the gods are in the genitive, which is rare in these images, where the nominative is the usual form. It is probably necessary to understand these inflected forms as if the genitive serves to complete the implied term *eikon:* "the image of Zeus," "the image of Hera," etc. In placing an inscription next to each figure, the painter makes

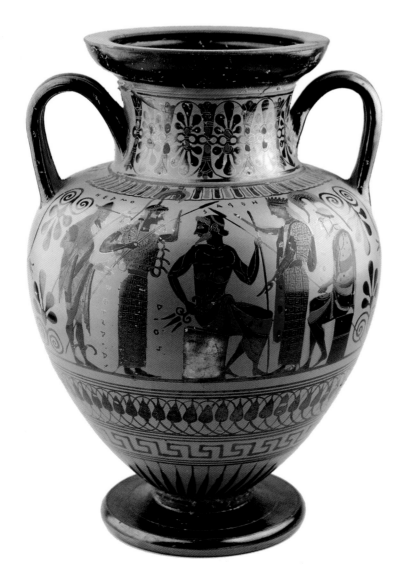

112. ATTIC BLACK-FIGURE AMPHORA
THREE LINES GROUP
520 BC, HEIGHT 0.29 M
PARIS, CABINET DES MÉDAILLES, BIBLIOTHÈQUE NATIONALE

perceptible both the visual and the sonorous presence of the gods whom he portrays; to read their name is in a way to invoke them.

With this assembly of gods serenely arranged around Zeus one can contrast the violence of the battle which pitted the Olympians against the giants, the sons of Gaia (the Earth) who gave them birth so that the Titans could have their vengeance. The giants launch an assault on Olympus, and the gods push them back with the help of Herakles. The representations of this combat, the Gigantomachy, are more numerous in sculpture than in ceramics, because it is a motif often taken up for the decoration of temples. The vase painters multiplied the images of group combat as well as of certain individual duels, such as that of Athena against Encelados or of Dionysos against Eurytos.

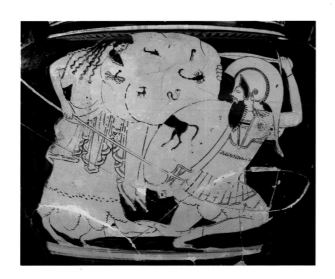

On a krater from around 480 BC that is now in Vienna, Poseidon confronts a giant who is armed like a hoplite, with a helmet, breastplate, greaves, and a round shield. He brandishes a sword, but has already fallen to his knees before the assault of Poseidon. His glassy eye without a marked pupil undoubtedly indicates his coming death. The god of the seas, armed with a trident, brandishes an enormous rock with which he prepares to overwhelm his adversary. In this extraordinary duel, the son of the Earth is defeated by the god who is not only the master of the marine waters but also one who makes the ground shake. The rock which he raises is a part of an island, a piece of the marine world. The painter has taken care to indicate in silhouette the terrestrial and marine animals which populate it: an octopus and a dolphin suggest the sea around the island, while a deer, a serpent, a kind of centipede and an enormous menacing scorpion animate its savage and rocky space.

This heavy mass comes to crush the giant and his shield, which is decorated in silhouette with a coat-of-arms: the tail-end of a horse accompanied by an inscription *kalos,* evoking the beauty of the cavalry and the aristocratic forms of war of which the savage duel between the god and the giant is a negation. Graphically, by this play of images which puts a secondary image within a primary one, a whole animal universe comes swarming in between the clashing faces of Poseidon and his adversary. The painter, in his way, makes perceptible the confusion of space, land and convulsing sea, and the violence of a cosmic battle which results in the triumph of the Olympian order, of which the preceding image manifested the sovereignty.

A HERO FOR ALL DANGERS 7

Herakles is definitely the most famous of Greek heroes. In the entire Attic output, he is the most often represented mythological figure. His numerous exploits have seduced the painters and their public, opening the way to innumerable variations on the well known as well as the more exotic scenes, which are linked to the more rare and therefore more surprising episodes.

One could not account here in detail for all this iconographic richness, no more than one would seek to present in one single chapter a brief narrative of this indefatigable hero. Since it is a matter of paying attention to each object and to each image in its singularity, we will try instead – without neglecting the background which makes them intelligible – to follow closely the specific characteristics of a limited number of representations, beginning with an exceptional drinking vase in the form of the head of Herakles.

The art of the potters did not limit itself to throwing vases; they were also modellers and some of their production is closer to sculpture than to pottery. This is the case with a small number of vases which take on the appearance of a human or an animal head. The selection of human figures found in this series is noteworthy, because it is clearly limited. The most frequent are women, as well as barbarians from Africa, for whom the potters took advantage of black glaze in order to represent these "black figures" in a new genre. These were the people who were considered subordinate according to Greek standards, in comparison to man in his identity as a citizen, whom one does not find in this series. At the other end of the spectrum, outside the human, one meets two masculine figures, one near the other: Herakles and Dionysos. Both are linked to wine and to drinking: Dionysos opened the way for men in this regard and Herakles is himself a great drinker. One remembers his meeting with the centaur Pholos and the opening of the jar of wine (fig. 27).

▶ 115. ATTIC RED-FIGURE KANTHAROS, SYRISKOS PAINTER
490 BC, HEIGHT 0.21 M
PARIS, CABINET DES MÉDAILLES, BIBLIOTHÈQUE NATIONALE

On this vase in the shape of a head, Herakles wears the lion skin which almost always identifies him. The paws of the animal are tied around the neck of the hero, whose face is framed by the lion's jaws. The fangs of the beast stand out against the hair, the beard and the cheeks of Herakles. High vertical handles rise from this head: they are characteristic of the form called *kantharos* (as opposed to the cup whose handles are horizontal). This form is rarely used by everyday drinkers, but it is often in the hands of Dionysos or of Herakles and one can say that in a certain way the hero is here an equivalent of his own vase.

116. REVERSE OF KANTHAROS, FIGURE 115

On the area which decorates the neck of this *kantharos* one recognizes another use of wine which we have already encountered: the libation. A winged goddess, Iris or Nike, pours the liquid into the phiale of a seated man, while a young man who is standing also holds out his phiale.

On the other side is the figure of a woman. This double head – Janus-like – does not however constitute a divine couple, for nothing allows us to recognize in this woman the feminine partner of Herakles, whether human or divine: she is neither Deianeira nor Omphale, still less Hebe, the personification of Youth, whom Herakles received in marriage when he entered Olympus. This has to do rather with that combination of a play on the different forms of otherness, in relation to the identity of a masculine drinker who uses this vase at the banquet: the hero is on one side, the woman on the other, this side and that, the superman and the feminine.

In the hands of the potter, Herakles takes shape; very quickly he is shown to us as he is, outside of all heroic action. Associated with wine, he is the drinking vase.

But more often Herakles acts; he seems indefatigable, even from his most tender youth. Herakles is the result of one of the many amorous adventures of Zeus with a mortal: the beautiful and faithful Alcmene, the wife of Amphitryon, the king of Thebes. She did not allow herself to be easily approached, and in order to come near, Zeus had to adopt the appearance of Amphitryon, who was away at war, while Hermes who accompanied him adopted that of the king's servant Sosias (Double). Therefore, this story of doubles is also a story of dual personalities. In effect, Alcmene receives in the course of the same night the man whom she takes for her husband, Zeus, but also Amphitryon, returned from the war at the same moment. In this way, she conceives twins: one is Herakles, the son of Zeus, and the other is Iphikles, the son of Amphitryon. The birth of twins is always a marvel; it emphasizes in this case the double nature of Herakles: divine by his father and mortal by his mother, which makes him a hero in the full sense, while Iphikles is but a mere mortal.

The Berlin painter gives a partial account of this play of doubles in a scene which shows the first exploit of the child Herakles. Jealous of the infidelities of Zeus, Hera, his divine wife, sought to eliminate this newborn who was not yet named Herakles but Alcides, from the name of his human grandfather Alkaios (which signifies Strength). She sent snakes to do this, to suffocate him in his crib. On the *stamnos* in the

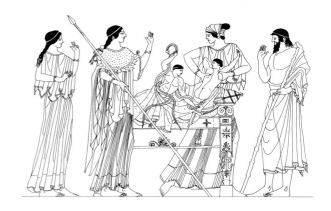

117. ATTIC RED-FIGURE STAMNOS, BERLIN PAINTER
480 BC, HEIGHT 0.51 M
PARIS, LOUVRE
118. DRAWING OF STAMNOS, FIGURE 117.

Louvre, the divine child battles with two snakes, while his twin Iphikles, seen from the back, seeks refuge in the arms of his mother who has come to take them away from danger. In the foreground and at the foot of the bed, occupying a place opposite that of Alcmene, Athena, who is armed with a lance, displays a gesture of astonishment, much like that of the bearded man on the right, who is without doubt Amphitryon. The place which Athena holds is noteworthy, because she makes herself if not a mother then at least a close protector of the young hero, for whose career she takes responsibility. Daughter of Zeus and therefore half-sister of Herakles, she accompanies him from his beginnings.

The other side of the vase shows Zeus framed by Hermes and Iris, both bearers of the caduceus, ready to rush forward, perhaps to spread the news of the glory of Herakles.

Pindar, in an ode in honor of the victor of a chariot race remembers this first battle: "In his two invincible hands he seized the neck of the two serpents."[1] Amphitryon comes brandishing his sword, and then stops, seized with astonishment. He questions the divine Tiresias. Pindar continues: "The latter explained to him, before the whole gathering, what destinies awaited Herakles; how many ferocious beasts he would slaughter on earth; how many he would slaughter in the sea; how he would bring the most frightful death to more than one man led by pride away from the correct path. Similarly, he revealed to him that when the

1. Pindar, *Nemean Odes,* I, 44-45 and 61-72.

119. METOPES AT THE TEMPLE OF ZEUS, MARBLE
460 BC, HEIGHT OF EACH METOPE 1.60 M
OLYMPIA, MUSEUM

gods…would wage war against the giants, the latter, under the blows of his arrows, would dirty their shining hair with the earth.

Then eternally in peace he would obtain, in recompense for his hard labors, the privilege of an unchanging happiness, in the home of the blessed; he would receive in marriage the vibrant Hebe, and living near Zeus the son of Cronos, would give thanks for his noble law."

In two stanzas, Pindar, through the prophetic voice of Tiresias, foretells the entire career of the hero, first on the earth, then among the gods, because, since he is of two natures, Herakles will have a double status, that of a hero among mortals and of a god among the Olympians.

In his evocation, the divine Tiresias remains very evasive and does not explain in much detail the exploits of Herakles, which would take a long time to enumerate. He contents himself with general categories: the animals on earth and in the sea, then the monsters, and finally the giants, the enemies of the Olympian gods. Such an evocation does not imply a rigorous order, and there exist many variations in the tale of the exploits of Herakles. We are today accustomed to speaking of the twelve labors as if they formed a fixed and well-ordered ensemble. But such a vision is late; one finds it in the erudite Alexandrians and with the historians who sought to systematize mythology for the benefit of ancient readers. In the 6th and 5th centuries BC the traditions concerning these labors were already very pliant, admitting many local variations.

The first arrangement of these labors in twelve episodes, around 460 BC, is found at the temple of Zeus in Olympia. The scheme of decoration, which is divided into twelve metopes, forced the sculptors to organize the exploits of the son of Zeus into a homogenous cycle. One finds the following labors: the Nemean lion, the hydra of Lerna, the Stymphalian birds, the Cretan bull, the deer of Ceryneia, the queen of the Amazons, the Erymanthian boar, the horses of Diomedes, the cattle of Geryon, the golden apples of the Hesperides, Cerberus the dog, and the stables of Augias.

Herakles is at home in Olympia, since it was there that he founded, in honor of his father, the Olympic Games, *athla*. The exploits of Herakles are themselves also called *athla,* and from this point of view one can consider Herakles as the athlete *par excellence.*

Some rare images concerning the education of Herakles seem to indicate that between the two parts of Greek culture, of the *paideia* of the young man, which is both musical and athletic, Herakles did not know how to maintain an equilibrium: he is completely on the side of the *athlon,* almost entirely abandoning musical culture. This is, in any case, what is shown by a small series of representations from the first half of the 5th century BC, in which the hero, still an adolescent, attacks his music teacher, Linos. On a cup from around 470 BC, a naked and beardless Herakles waves a chair above Linos in order to hit him on the head; the teacher is not seated on an ordinary chair, but on an altar, in the manner of a supplicant. As a result, he resembles Priam put to death by Neoptolemos (fig. 86), which accentuates the brutality and the impiety of Herakles. The staff at the left suggests that the hero may have been hit and is reacting violently, while the writing case above Linos indicates his function as schoolmaster.

120. ATTIC RED-FIGURE CUP, STIEGLITZ PAINTER
470 BC, MAXIMUM DIAMETER 0.33 M
PARIS, CABINET DES MÉDAILLES, BIBLIOTHÈQUE NATIONALE

Even if Herakles later on became a cithara player, like the musicians in the competitions, the son of Zeus does not seem made for school, nor for the urban and civic life. He travels the world, starting with his region of Thebes, and especially with Argos, where his cousin Eurystheus ruled. Herakles, in order to cleanse himself of the murder of the children whom he had with Megara, which he committed after a fit of foolishness sent by Hera, had to atone for his sin. He therefore placed himself in the service of Eurystheus, the king of Mycenae and of Tiryns, and the protégé of Hera.

Encouraged by the goddess, the king of Mycenae imposed upon Herakles seemingly impossible tests, over which the hero managed to triumph each time. These twelve years of servitude are marked by twelve labors whose order varies, but which always begin with the victory over the Nemean lion, in the north of the Peloponnese. This exploit is by far the most frequently represented, because it gives at the outset the measure of Herakles' abnormal strength. The Nemean lion is not an ordinary lion; it is a monster whose origin Hesiod recalls in his *Theogony:* it descended from Echidna (the Viper), half woman, half serpent, mother of a whole series of monsters, many of whom were adversaries of Herakles: "Typhon fell in love with her…She first brought Orthos, the dog of Geryon, into the world. After him she gave birth to another irresistible monster, which one scarcely dares name, the cruel Cerberus, the dog of Hades…and after that one, she brought the Hydra into the world, who knew only atrocious deeds, the monster of Lerna, which Hera the white-armed made grow in order to satisfy her appalling hate for Herakles the strong...She also gave birth to Chimaera...the one whom Pegasus chased, bringing triumph to the valiant Bellerophon. She also gave birth, after having submitted to the law of Orthos, to Phix the wicked one, which was a disaster for the Cadmeans, and to the Nemean lion, which the noble wife of Zeus, Hera, made grow in the Nemean valleys, the scourge of humans. There he decimated the people of the goddess...But he perished under the vigorous arm of Herakles the strong."[2]

2. Hesiod, *Theogony,* 306-332.

If the Chimaera is fought by Bellerophon and the Phix (similar to the Sphinx) is defeated by Oedipus, the other children of Echidna seem created for Herakles and supported by the vindictiveness of Hera. In this series the lion, with his sister the Sphinx, occupies a particular place, since he is the son of Echidna and Orthos, a son of Echidna himself. In this incestuous short-circuit is inscribed the monstrosity of this lion which, far from being an ordinary animal, combines in his origins woman, serpent, and dog.

Nothing could come near this invulnerable beast, neither fire nor sword. No weapon could pierce him; thus Herakles had to relinquish his bow and his sword and confront the animal with his bare hands.

On a lekythos attributed to the Diosphos painter, the hero braces himself, knee to the ground, about to strangle the lion. The animal is immobilized, jaws open, tongue hanging out, pinned to the ground by Herakles who holds him in a powerful grip. The black silhouette of the lion contrasts with the muscular body of the hero, drawn in a simple outline. This technique, which comes from black-figure painting, highlights the contrast between man and animal. The naked body of Herakles, who has hung his clothing as well as his sword on the branches of a tree standing in the background, is treated like that of an athlete: his posture corresponds more to that of a wrestler than that of a hunter. His exploit has nothing to do with the hunt, but is athletic. In relinquishing his bow and sword, Herakles confronts the lion as he confronts the giant Antaeus, hand to hand. The tension in the arms and thigh of the hero corresponds to the effort of the lion who pushes his back paw in vain against the head of Herakles in order to free himself. The lion is taken and will suffocate.

Having come out the winner of this battle, Herakles appropriates the lion skin for himself to make it an invulnerable protection. After this first exploit, Herakles will always be seen in the jaws of the lion, from

which he takes all his savage strength. While certain heroes – Achilles for example – wear on their shields a lion which metaphorically expresses their aggressive strength (fig. 84), Herakles does without this defense and fits directly upon his body the invulnerable skin of the son of Echidna. Through this the hero makes himself an animal, while in the battle the lion becomes human.

On a small red-figure pelike, the Geras painter chose to show the moment when Herakles is about to dress himself in the lion skin. He holds it spread out before him by the back paws; the head hangs down, lifeless, eyes closed, jaws cracked open in the middle to fit the face of the hero. In the center of the image the club is set at an angle, while Herakles looks to the left at a bearded athlete who seems to be warming up. His size is colossal; his arm extends onto the ornamental frieze which marks the top of the painting. Perhaps he is the giant Antaeus, son of the Earth, whom Herakles must suffocate, a bit like the Nemean lion, but by raising him off the ground, because he regains his strength only by touching the soil. The unusual moment chosen by the painter compares this scene with the athletic images representing the young men in the palaestra. This impression is confirmed by the other side of the vase where a Hermes-column is seen, to which a young man in a cloak offers a prayer in touching him on the beard. This type of statue, which marks entrances and passages, often distinguishes the palaestra of which Hermes is a familiar god. More than the exploit and the effort of the hero, the painter is interested here in the athletic image of a Herakles who could serve as the mythical model for the Athenian wrestler.

122, 123. ATTIC RED-FIGURE PELIKE, GERAS PAINTER
490 BC, HEIGHT 0.20 M
PARIS, CABINET DES MÉDAILLES, BIBLIOTHÈQUE NATIONALE

124, 125. ATTIC BLACK-FIGURE LEKYTHOS, DIOSPHOS PAINTER
500-490 BC, HEIGHT 0.22 M
PARIS, LOUVRE

But let us take up again the exploits of Herakles. On the cylindrical lekythoi from the end of the 6th century BC, as well as on the small late black-figure amphoras, the Diosphos and Sappho painters, who belonged to the same workshop, expanded on these types of representation. One exploit per vase, with favorite themes and with rarities. The idea of a cycle – comparable to that which one finds a bit later on the metopes of Olympia – appears only with the first red-figures, on large vases, and remains exceptional.

On a lekythos by the Diosphos painter, Herakles battles the Hydra of Lerna. Like the Nemean lion, she is born of Echidna, but has for her father Typhon, the son of Gaia (the Earth) and Tartaros. Just as Echidna is half-woman, half-serpent, Typhon has a monstrous body:

3. Hesiod, *Theogony*, 824-26.

"From his shoulders rose one hundred serpent heads, and horrible dragons, shooting out blackish tongues."[3]

One is not, then, surprised by the result; the Hydra is described as a serpent with many heads, from five to one hundred, according to various authors. On the vase in the Louvre, Herakles is grappling with a sort of swarming mass, a knot of vipers, from which one makes out a thick body which ends in a double tail, and from which emerge, like a bouquet of tentacles, eight or nine serpent-shaped bodies. The son of Zeus has grabbed one of these tentacles, as he had already done in the cradle. But here it is not just a matter of strangling the beast, because he would have to hold all the heads at once. Herakles is armed with a sort of sickle, a *harpe* (the same weapon which Perseus used to decapitate the Gorgon), in order to slice into the living flesh and sever the heads. However, the test does not end there, because the heads reproduce themselves as soon as they are severed; to put an end to this incessant self-begetting, one must immediately cauterize the wound so that nothing can grow from it. This is what was done by Iolaos, the faithful companion of Herakles, whose arm, opposite that of the hero, we see holding one of the serpents. In his left hand he waves a brand lit in the fire which burns behind him on the ground, on the other side of the vase. In order to confront this many-sided monster, one needs at the same time both the fire and the sword, which were of no use against the Nemean lion. Herakles cannot, for once, act alone; the help of Iolaos is indispensable in completing the labor. Right away Hera sends a second adversary against Herakles. Between the legs of the hero is an enormous crab standing on monstrous claws, while Athena, with her extended arm covered by her aegis, stands behind Herakles. The crab *(carcinos)* crushed by the hero would become, according to some authors, the constellation Cancer.

On this simple lekythos, in a reduced space, the Diosphos painter knew how to show the monstrous swarm of the beast and the invincible energy of the hero, supported as usual by his half-sister Athena.

The same painter treated, on a small amphora in the Louvre, a later episode in the deeds of Herakles, that of the Stymphalian birds in Arcadia, in the heart of the Peloponnese. This theme is very rare in Attic imagery. The nature of these birds varies according to sources, but all say that their number made them unbearable in the region. While, according to Strabo,[4] Herakles would make them leave the forest in which they had taken cover by frightening them with a

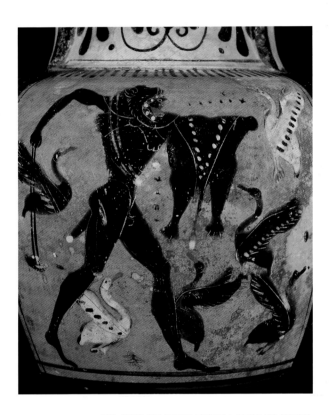

126. ATTIC RED-FIGURE AMPHORA, DIOSPHOS PAINTER
500 BC. HEIGHT 0.20 M
PARIS, LOUVRE

4. Strabo, *Geography*, VIII, 6, 8-371.

tambourine, in order to shoot them down with his arrows, the Diosphos painter presents another version.

Herakles advances among the birds, naked, sword at his side; his head is covered by the jaws of the lion and the front paws of the beast are tied around his neck while the rest of the skin hangs over his extended left arm. He thus protects himself against the birds, four of which are black and two white, and web-footed with menacing beaks. In his right hand he holds a sling loaded with a heavy stone. In the background, a series of formless letters, which lack any meaning, assure in a way a resonant composition. On the other side Iolaos, also armed with a sling, battles against five other birds. In this version, Herakles behaves like a hunter, using a new type of weapon for him, the sling, which is hardly heroic.

One can compare this motif with the scene which decorates the foot of the François vase. The Pygmies also battle a swarm of birds, the cranes, scourge of Greek farmers, which have come in their migration to attack the tiny people. Some among them are armed with slings, just like Herakles. But the scales are not the same; while these birds dominate the poor Pygmies, Herakles, standing solidly on his feet, with arms spread wide, easily gets the better, once again, of the swarm of winged creatures which surrounds him.

The first six labors of Herakles take place in the Peloponnese, but such a narrow geographic area is not large enough for such a hero. Not content to rid mainland Greece of the monsters which infest it, he crosses the seas and surveys savage lands in order to confront new monsters and new forms of savagery, which each time he successfully eliminates or subdues. Thus he is able for a while to calm the fury of the Cretan bull, to tame the man-eating horses of Diomedes, the king of Thrace, and to seize the girdle of Hippolyta, the queen of the Amazons. Other labors take him even farther away, to the limits of the inhabited world, towards the West in particular since it was his duty, always on behalf of Eurystheus, to seize Geryon's herd of cattle. These fall into the same monstrous genealogy as the Nemean lion and the hydra of Lerna, since he descended, like Echidna, from Phorkys and Keto. He is the son of Chrysaor, himself born of the Gorgon Medusa. Let us listen once more to Hesiod: "Chrysaor engendered the three-headed Geryon, united with Callihroe, daughter of the illustrious Oceanos. Herakles-the-strong killed the latter near his cattle with the crooked gait, in Erythia, which is surrounded by waves, the day when he pushed his cattle with the broad

127. ATTIC RED-FIGURE KRATER, DETAIL OF FOOT, KLEITIAS
570 BC, HEIGHT 0.66 M
FLORENCE, ARCHAEOLOGICAL MUSEUM

5. Hesiod, *Theogony,* 287-294.

foreheads towards the holy Tirynts, after having leapt over the Ocean and killed both Orthos and Eurytion the cattleman, together in their misty field, beyond the illustrious Ocean."[5] The isle of Erythia, where Geryon resides, is found beyond the Ocean, on the edges of the western world. To get himself there, Herakles has no other way but to follow the course of the sun which sets every evening at this extremity of the world and to cross the Ocean in a cup which brings him to the Orient.

The Sappho painter tries to give an idea of this mythic geography on a lekythos which links Herakles with the Sun. The hero is stopped in route, on the summit of a mountain marked by a thick, winding black band. He is squatting and roasting some meat on a spit over the flame of an altar. Below him a dog lies down on the ground and turns around; it has sometimes been interpreted as Cerberus, the guardian of the Underworld, but nothing makes him the frightening monster which we know from other images. Perhaps what we have here is a dog on the look-out for some meat to fall from Herakles' feast.

When one turns the vase, an astonishing quasi-cosmological composition is discovered. At the center of the scene, on the lower part of the image, a chariot drawn by four horses abreast and seen head-on emerges from the horizon; it is driven by an *auriga,* a charioteer, above whom appears a disk with a luminous crown and an inscription: *Helios,* "the Sun." We see then that, suddenly appearing out of the Ocean, the Sun is moving through the sky. Above him, symmetrically arranged in profile, are two harnessed teams of horses who soar upwards from behind a large band marked with white embellishments which could indicate waves or thick clouds. The chariot on the left is driven by a woman named *Nuxs,* "Night," and the one on the right by *Eos,* "Dawn." The chariot of the Sun is therefore associated with the image of Day and Night, of daily time to whose duration the Sun gives rhythm. Full-face and profile combine on the cylindrical surface of the vase to make perceptible this astronomical period.

If the design allows us to better understand the graphic organization of such a composition, we must not forget that this image is in fact cylindrical and can only be grasped in its entirety by turning the vase, making real by this gesture the duration of the day which unfolds in its particularity under the eyes of the viewer. One catches sight of Herakles, near the Sun, on the far shores of the Ocean, on his way to the isle of Geryon, seeking to obtain the help of Helios for his journey.

▶ **128.** ATTIC BLACK-FIGURE LEKYTHOS, SAPPHO PAINTER
490 BC, HEIGHT 0.17 M
NEW YORK, METROPOLITAN MUSEUM

129. FULL VIEW OF VASE, FIGURE 128

The confrontation between Herakles and Geryon is a frequent theme in archaic painting. We know more than 130 examples of it, the majority of which are Attic; but the theme was also of interest to one of the vase painters established in Magna Graecia, without doubt near the Strait of Messina, to whom is attributed the production of the vases incorrectly called "Chalcidian," because they bear inscriptions using the alphabet standard in Chalcis, in Euboea. Painters coming from Euboea, an island to the north-east of Attica, revived the tradition of Athenian black-figure painting and developed it in the western part of the Greek world. On an amphora belonging to this group, the adventure of Herakles in the west spreads out over the entire circumference of the vase.

The monster Geryon is present here with a multiple body: three heads, three torsos, three pairs of arms, but only one pelvis and one pair of legs. He is not simply three-headed, as Hesiod said he was, but far more many-faceted, to the point of adopting, when facing Heracles, the appearance of a rank of heavily armed Hoplites. Moreover, while Hesiod gives the monster a name in the singular – *Geryonea* – the inscription which appears in front of them on the vase designates them in the plural – *Garywones*. The monster is also equipped with a pair of wings which are echoed on the coat of arms of the first shield, on which appears a predatory bird with wings spread. On the earth lie the cattleman Eurytion and his dog, which is not named (but known elsewhere as Orthos). Herakles has killed them and now threatens the triple Geryon with his bow; one of his arrows is stuck in the back of Eurytion, another in the neck of the monster. Behind the hero, the lance-bearing Athena encourages him with a gesture; the serpents which border her aegis spread themselves widely around her, giving her a more menacing air than in contemporary Attic images. Further to the left, Geryon's herd – five oxen in a compact group – await the fate in store for them, while Iolaos, upright on a chariot and seen head-on, stands ready to leave with his master.

◄ **130.** CHALCIDIAN BLACK-FIGURE AMPHORA
INSCRIPTIONS PAINTER
540 BC, HEIGHT 0.41 M
PARIS, CABINET DES MÉDAILLES, BIBLIOTHÈQUE NATIONALE

131. FULL VIEW OF VASE, FIGURE 130

The chariot, as well as the heavy armor of Geryon – helmet, shield, and greaves – return us to a type of war in which Herakles is clearly preeminent. He fights with bow, like a hunter, and at a distance (even if the composition puts the bow held by the hero in contact with the shields of his adversaries, therefore eliminating the trajectories of the arrows). The use of such a weapon in no way diminishes the valor of Herakles' exploits, but rather it indicates again that the monster Geryon is a hunted animal.

It is rare that the adversaries of Herakles would be comparable to "normal" warrior figures like the Amazons, who are, however, both women and barbarians – or like Cycnos, the son of Ares. In most cases the son of Zeus, the lion-headed hero, confronts monstrous and wicked animals, who are combinations of creatures, or else are among the many creatures who cannot find their place in the world of the city. A civilizing hero, Herakles is certainly also an extraordinary hero. It is this profound difference which allows him to go so far in his wanderings outside the Greek world. Not only to the boundaries of the Ocean, but even to the underground world which is ruled by Hades the Invisible. The hero finds himself in effect set with the task of bringing back from the Underworld the dog Cerberus, whose identity we know as a son of Echidna.

Like Geryon, Cerberus has three heads, or three bodies; but to this body of a dog is added the tail of a serpent. To succeed in seizing him, Herakles needs the help of Hermes and Athena. First he introduces himself to the mysteries of Eleusis, in order to escape the fear of death. Once he arrives in the Underworld, which Cerberus guards, the hero obtains from Hades permission to take the monster away, on the condition that he not use any of his weapons. It is therefore once again the strength in his arms which allows him to restrain the dog, and to lead it on a leash to the home of King Eurystheus.

On a hydria in the Ionian tradition, possibly produced in Caere (Cerveteri) in Etruria, the painter has represented not without malice the moment of arrival at the palace of Eurystheus. The king, panicked, takes refuge in a large jar, a *pithos,* which serves as a shelter. Frightened, he raises his hands in the air when he sees the monster, which is led by Herakles at the end of a long chain. The animal stands on its hind legs, all mouths open and fangs menacing. The painter has used a richer polychromy than that of Attic black-figure painting in order to display the spread of the three heads of Cerberus, which are

132. BLACK-FIGURE HYDRIA FROM CAERE, PAINTER OF THE CAERETAN HYDRIAE
530 BC, HEIGHT 0.43 M
PARIS, LOUVRE

successively white, red, and black, and haloed with a whole series of
serpents pointing at the frightened king.

Eurystheus did not know what to do with such a catch and Cerberus
was returned to Hades. With this exploit, and the acquisition of the
golden apples of the garden of the Hesperides, ends the series of the
labors of Herakles.

But the hero does not rest there. Aside from the various adventures
parallel to the principal labors, the long story of the exploits of
Herakles contains many other episodes. Attic imagery does not treat
all of them; the play of local variants, through which each city and
each region of the Greek world seeks to appropriate the glory of the
hero, favors such developments, upon which we cannot linger here.

However, the end of the story of Herakles requires that we stop
here, because it held the interest of the image-makers of Athens and
poses once again the question of his double nature – heroic and
divine. There exist, in effect, a certain number of images which are not
related to the cycle of the labors, but which put Herakles in contact
with various figures of the Olympian pantheon.

On a bell-shaped krater from the end of the 5th century BC, a naked
Herakles, with his club on his shoulder, is riding on a chariot driven by a
woman with outspread wings, Nike, or Victory. The horses, which are
white and red, parade behind the god Hermes, who is to the left,
recognized by his white caduceus. This god who is both a herald and a
messenger, the one who leads both the parade of newlyweds as well as the
funeral procession, leads the movement of the hero, but there is nothing

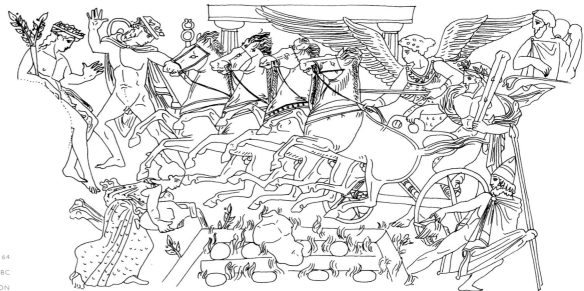

in the image to indicate from where he comes or where he is going. Two columns appear above the horses, suggesting a portico, a constructed space of a very generic manner. The victorious Herakles passes by.

One can make this reading clear by comparing this krater to another contemporary example found in Sant' Agata dei Goti, near Naples, which is today in a private collection. One finds on it the same composition which is on the upper part of this image: Herakles and Nike on a chariot, preceded by Hermes, topped by two columns in the background. But there is more here. On the lower register, under the chariot, one sees at the left a woman who pours water from a hydria onto a pyre which is still in flames. To the right a bearded man moves away, with two lances in his left hand and a quiver in his right. These particular elements, especially the pyre – which is rare in the Attic repertoire – when associated with Herakles, bring us back to the moment of the hero's death.

Deianeira, betrayed by her husband Herakles, who preferred Iole, offered to the hero a tunic soaked in the blood and semen of the centaur Nessos. The latter, who had tried to rape Deianeira, told her, at the moment of his death from the blows of Herakles, a deceitful secret. He suggested this mixture to her, this *pharmakon,* which she took to be a remedy but which was only a poison, and promised her that his tunic, soaked in such a potion, would ensure, if the need arose, the fidelity of her husband.

As soon as he was dressed in this tunic of death which stuck to his skin and which he could not remove, Herakles experienced unbearable burns. He wanted only one thing: to die immediately. Philoctetes agreed to help him, erecting a pyre upon which the hero stretched out and which he lit. Such a suicide serves as a funeral ritual, except that Herakles, devoured by the poisoned fire of the centaur, is still living at the moment when the flames of the pyre consume him.

Once everything is consumed, the usual ritual requires that one extinguish the flames and then collect the ashes or bones of the deceased in an urn or a vase, in order to bury them in the ground. In the case of Herakles, nothing was found on the pyre except his weapons. The rest of his mortal body disappeared without a trace.

The painter, to indicate this absence and make it visible, represented on the pyre a simple anatomic breastplate which resembles a torso without head or arms, a sort of empty shell. The body of the hero who died on the pyre is nothing but a hollow cast, while in the upper register, the naked Herakles whom Nike accompanies has already passed to the side of the gods.

Therefore it is truly a matter of an apotheosis, of a transformation into a god. This rite of passage, which for mortals, as it takes place by means of funerals, leads the living to the dead, and the visible to the invisible, is transformed here into a process which makes the body of the mortal hero invisible in order to better make visible his divine immortal image.

The skin of the lion which usually covers the hero and makes him invulnerable is replaced on the pyre by an anatomical breastplate, which is even better for making evident the bodily transformation of the hero who has become a god. The quiver which Philoctetes takes away, at the level of the ground, is that of the archer hero; the handing down of the weapons on earth is certain (as in the case of the weapons of Achilles); they pass from the dead to the living, from the hero Herakles to Philoctetes.

Herakles the god has kept only his club, now carried like a scepter, a sign of his strength and his divine power. The mortal hero, the son of Alcmene, has disappeared on the pyre, while the immortal god, the son of Zeus, is brought on a chariot which leads him among the Olympians: one will notice the presence of Apollo, crowned with laurel, seated in the upper left of the scene.

The double nature of Herakles is clearly indicated in this image which uses the double register to set in opposition the absent corpse and the triumphant body. The painter was successful in concretizing the paradox which Pindar expresses in an enigmatic summary, since he names Herakles as the *heros theos,* "hero-god";[6] not a hero and then a god, but hero and god at the same time. This paradox finds its confirmation in the way in which the cult of Herakles is organized in

6. Pindar, *Nemean Odes III,* 22.

certain cities, as well as the recollection of Herodotus, on the subject of Thasos, an isle in the north of the Aegean Sea: "The wisest Greeks are those who have two different sanctuaries dedicated to two Herakles' and sacrifice to one as to an immortal who is an Olympian, but give to the other the worship owing to a hero."[7]

This same double nature of Herakles, made explicit in the organization of the cults in Thasos, is clearly indicated by the separation of the pyre and the chariot on the krater of Sant'Agata dei Goti. On the Vienna krater, this theme remains implicit. Only the triumph of Herakles, guided by Hermes and Nike, is shown by the painter. It is left to the viewer to mentally restore the point of earthly departure of such a journey from Oeta to Olympus. The image constructed in this way remains open, as do many images on vases, which proceed more often by allusion and ellipsis than in an explicit and detailed manner.

Many scenes which feature Herakles remain allusive. We see him next to a divinity without it being possible – or even necessary – to say whether he is a hero or a god. Essentially, we must follow Pindar and consider him a hero-god. Two examples, among many others, will allow us to clarify this aspect.

On a small amphora attributed to the Diosphos painter – the same one to which he owes his name – there appears on one side Hera standing in front of the seated Zeus, who holds on his knees a small child accompanied by a problematic inscription, *Diosphos,* to which we must

7. Herodotus, *The Histories,* II, 44.

135. ATTIC BLACK-FIGURE AMPHORA, DIOSPHOS PAINTER
500-490 BC, HEIGHT 0.25 M
PARIS, CABINET DES MÉDAILLES, BIBLIOTHÈQUE NATIONALE

return later (fig. 135). On the other side, which is the one that interests us here, we see Herakles, on the right, turning around towards Athena. The goddess wears the aegis, holds a lance in her right hand and her helmet in her left, as if to salute the hero. In front of her an ox suggests the sacrifices in honor of the Poliad, the goddess who is the keeper of the city. We have often seen Athena next to Herakles, whom she constantly helps in his exploits. A goddess in her own right, she is also the daughter of Zeus. The presence of the ruler of Olympus on the obverse of the vase recalls this double paternity; the joint presence of Hera, who most often persecuted the very one who ended up bearing her name in order to tell his glory – *Hera kles* – suggests all the tensions and conflicts which were imposed upon the hero during this long series of labors. However, no exploit of Herakles is represented here, no trial is shown. The simple combination of the two paintings, Zeus and Hera surrounding Diosphos on one side, Athena and Herakles on the other, suggests to the viewer a combination of figures which condenses in its way many of the events linked with the paternity of Zeus. The child who stands on his knee is in effect Dionysos, son of Zeus and Semele. We have then, combined on the same vase, the sacred couple of Olympus, Zeus and Hera, but also three children of Zeus, Dionysos, Athena, and Herakles, who each represent a different mode of birth and of belonging to the Olympian pantheon. In this ensemble, Herakles is the most marginal, the most rooted in a heroic humanity of which Dionysos shares certain traits that bring him closer to his half-brother.

These two sons of Zeus are both born of a Theban princess. However, Dionysos, son of Semele, was not carried to term by his mother. Advised by the jealous Hera, she wished to be able to see Zeus in all his splendor, and she then perished, struck by lightning on seeing him. Zeus then carried in his thigh the child who was to come. Born of Zeus, he would be divine, while Herakles, brought into the world by Alcmene, is mortal.

The two half-brothers are often associated, in particular around wine or in the practice of the *symposion*. A cooling vase – a *psykter* – attributed to the Kleophrades painter gives us a remarkable example. In the foreground Herakles stands with club and bow in hand, facing Dionysos, who carries an ivy branch and a vase with vertical handles – a *kantharos* – which we have seen characterizes Herakles as well as Dionysos. Between them, standing on the ground in black silhouette, a second *kantharos* punctuates a long frieze of nine other drinking vases –

skyphoi – which are regularly spaced. The children of Zeus are placed under the symbol of wine and shared drinking.

On the upper register, a series of crouching satyrs, seen alternately from front and back, seem surprised, if not frightened, by this meeting. The companions of Dionysos seem afraid of the violence of Herakles, the hunter of monsters, who sometimes, indeed, did not spare them. But these encounters never result in a massacre; the satyrs are not centaurs. Certain commentators on this vase have considered that the line on which the satyrs go forward, with their perfectly rhythmical gestures, could indicate a stage set and their movements a choral dance. But nothing obliges us to interpret this image in a theatrical mode, even if the first design to be published (fig. 137, in the 1840's), by separating the satyrs from the two gods, gives the impression that the first ones, placed behind and not in front of the principal figures, dance around them, like the chorus below the theatrical stage. It is more important to note that the vase, made to be seen at the banquet, and dipped into a krater of mixed wine, represents the meeting of two figures of the Greek pantheon, one of whom, Herakles, is sometimes called *alexikakos,* "the one who rids us of evils," and the other, Dionysos, *lusimeles,* "the one who delivers us from worries."

Throughout this series of images one sees the development of a complex figure, always in action, fighting with all sorts of weapons – club, bow, sword, and sling – or with bare hands, against all kinds of monsters in which human and animal combine; sometimes paused, if never at rest, pictured in the act of associating with other divine figures of the pantheon, particularly Athena and Dionysos. These last two divinities occupy with Herakles an essential place in the repertoire of Attic vases, one because she is the Poliad goddess, the one who gives her name to the city of Athens, and the other because he made the gift of wine to men and for that finds a quasi-natural place on the drinking vases. It is therefore to these gods that we must now turn our gaze.

THE MYTHIC IDENTITY OF THE ATHENIANS 8

While the Greek gods are immortal, they are not the creators of the world. They belong to this world – formed from Chaos and from Gaia, the Earth – and must be born, sometimes not without pain. Dionysos and Athena both came out of the body of Zeus who engendered them, thus fulfilling the great fantasy of the Greeks: to give birth without women.

Athena is the daughter of Zeus and Metis (Intelligence), herself the daughter of Tethys and Oceanos. In the successive generations of gods, Zeus took the place of his father Cronos, who himself had taken the place of his own father, Ouranos. To avoid that a son would in turn replace him, Zeus, advised by Gaia, swallowed Metis: "He put her safely in his bowels."[1] Only the first daughter whom Metis carried was born: she is Athena.

The childbirth took a very particular turn. On a red-figure hydria, Zeus is enthroned at the center of the image, with a scepter and a phiale in his hands, symbols of the libations offered to him. Above his head leaps a feminine figure of reduced size, but already an adult. Athena comes out of the head of Zeus, "uttering a war cry," fully armed, brandishing a lance, with the aegis on her extended arm. In front of Zeus stands the god Hephaistos, a double axe in his hand; after having split the skull of the sovereign of Olympus, he makes a prudent retreat with a gesture of astonishment. This group is framed by two women, also amazed, without doubt the goddesses of childbirth, the Eilithyiai. To the left a winged woman, Nike, shows her surprise.

In the paradox of a divine birth which conforms neither to biological order nor to the temporality of humans, Zeus gives birth from above to a totally formed being. The armed Athena, born from her father, is not an infant; she is hardly feminine either, taking upon herself from the first day the emblems which make her a warrior. In this type of scene, which exists very early as an image, Athena often wears a helmet, and is equipped with a shield, as we see on certain bronze shield bands offered at the temple of Zeus at Olympia.

By inverting the values and the status of masculine and feminine – Zeus giving birth to a goddess who is an adult and who has manly qualities – the stories and images make Athena an exceptional figure in the midst of the pantheon, which justifies her role as the Poliad goddess, the protectress of the city. In effect, she gives her name to Athens, after having achieved sovereignty over Attica, against her rival Poseidon. The country until then bore the name of King Cecrops, or Cecropia, as Apollodoros recounts: "It was in his time that the gods decided to take

1. Hesiod, *Theogony*, 890.

139. ATTIC RED-FIGURE HYDRIA, PAINTER OF TARQUINA 707
470 BC, HEIGHT 0.37 M
PARIS, CABINET DES MÉDAILLES, BIBLIOTHÈQUE NATIONALE

140, 141. FULL VIEW AND DETAIL OF HYDRIA, FIGURE 139

142. ARGIVE BRONZE SHIELD BAND (DRAWING)
575-550 BC. HEIGHT 0.08 M
OLYMPIA, ARCHAEOLOGICAL MUSEUM

possession of the cities, in which each one would have a special cult. Poseidon was the first to come to Attica. By striking his trident in the middle of the Acropolis, he made a sea appear…After him came Athena. Taking Cecrops as a witness of her taking possession, she planted an olive tree…A dispute for the possession of the country rose up between the two divinities and Zeus summoned the twelve gods to judge. According to their verdict, the country was entrusted to Athena."[2]

The mythical topography of the Acropolis echoes such stories; on the inside of the Erechtheion is shown the "Erechtheion sea" as well as the olive tree of Athena in the orchard of Pandrosos. Not far from there, on the pediments of the Parthenon, which is consecrated to Athena *Parthenos*, the Virgin, these two essential moments are portrayed in sculpture: to the east the birth of Athena, and to the west her dispute with Poseidon.

2. Apollodoros, *Library,* III, 14.

143. ATTIC BLACK-FIGURE AMPHORA, SIGNED BY THE POTTER AMASIS
540 BC, HEIGHT 0.32 M
PARIS, CABINET DES MÉDAILLES, BIBLIOTHÈQUE NATIONALE

144, 145. ATTIC RED-FIGURE KRATER, NIKIAS PAINTER
410 BC, HEIGHT 0.38 M
RICHMOND, VIRGINIA MUSEUM

On an amphora signed by the potter Amasis there appear face-to-face Athena on the left and Poseidon on the right. The signature of the potter which runs along the length of Poseidon's trident emphasizes the regulated and controlled character of the composition, all the while marking a division between the two divinities. There is no agitation, no tension in this meeting in which Athena, with hand raised, greets the maritime god. The scene tells nothing; only the simultaneous presence of these two gods suggests the time of the origins of the city, where they enter into competition. But the conflicts are here erased, reserved for the humans who confront each other in warlike duels on the small frieze at the base of the neck. The change in scale and the position of this quasi-ornamental band highlight the contrast between the tumultuous world of men and the more peaceful vision of the meetings between gods.

On the other side, Dionysos, in an attitude equivalent to that of Athena, immobile and with hand raised, greets two dancing maenads, to which we will return. From one side to the other, the Amasis painter makes visible the relationship of the gods among themselves as well as the meeting between men and gods, around Dionysos, through wine and dance.

The stories of the Athenians concerning their own origins are complex and give an essential role to Athena. Given birth by her father, Athena is a virgin goddess, a helmeted and armed *parthenos* who refuses marriage. She is not less desirable for it; the blacksmith god Hephaistos, driven by strong desire, pursued her but could not join his body to hers. Only his semen reached the thigh of the goddess, who cleaned the stain by wiping it with a flock of wool which she then threw on the ground; it is from this ground that a child was born, Erichthonios, the future king of Athens.

The painters found original ways to narrate such a birth. On a krater from around 410 BC, Athena appears in the center, leaning forward, her right foot resting on a rock, taking into her arms the newborn whom Gaia, the Earth, holds out to her. Gaia, who wears a high crown, emerges from the ground which is marked by the horizontal line which hides her legs and her feet. This scheme of anodos, or emergence, makes real the passage from the subterranean world into the open air, the birth which is from out of the ground and not from a female womb, which allows the Athenians to call themselves *autochthon,* born of the earth, of their own soil. In this they compare themselves with many cities whose people, always according to the Athenians, come from elsewhere.

In this image, the painter used white embellishment not to indicate what

is feminine (as is the case in black-figure painting), but to give more brilliance to the infant Erichthonius, who passes from the hands of Gaia to those of Athena. All eyes are turned towards him: those of Hermes, in the upper left, partially hidden by a rock, and of Nike at the right, who, with wings spread, holds Athena's lance and shield; and also those of Hephaistos who leans on his staff in the lower left, and of Aphrodite, seated at the right, who aroused the passions of the blacksmith god. Farther away near the handles one finds Zeus standing on the right, behind Aphrodite, and an unidentified hero to the left of Apollo who is seated near a tripod.

Thus Gaia, the Earth, ensures, between Hephaistos and Athena, the sequence of events which will allow the birth of an infant who is *autochthon*. He will first be hidden in a basket entrusted to the daughters of Cecrops, then brought up on the Acropolis, before reigning over Athens and, among other things, founding the Panathenaia, which are the festivals in honor of Athena.

Erichthonios is one of the most complex figures among those whom we find at the beginnings of Athens, but he is not the only one. The list of local heroes who are scattered throughout the territory of Attica and the legends which are attached to them would be very long. The painters did not use all these motifs; certain figures have known considerable fame while others seem to be only curiosities for mythographers. By confining ourselves to images, we can see as major figures that of Triptolemos and especially that of Theseus, the one most frequently represented.

The story of Triptolemos is linked to the land of Eleusis, a large village to the west of Athens. When Persephone, the only daughter of Zeus and Demeter, was carried off by Hades and brought to the subterranean world where he resides, the tearful Demeter left in search of her daughter. After much wandering, she arrived exhausted in Eleusis and was welcomed by the parents of Triptolemos. To thank them for their hospitality, Demeter gave man the gift of wheat and entrusted to Triptolemos the task of spreading it throughout the world. Dionysios of Halicarnassos brings to mind one of the tragedies of Sophocles dedicated to this subject: "In it, he showed Demeter indicating to Triptolemos the entire expanse of the lands through which he had to travel in order to sow the seeds which she gave him." [3]

We know more than 120 vases upon which this motif appears. A krater attributed to the Hektor painter gives an exceptional version. To the right, the young Triptolemos is about to ascend a throne fitted with

3. Dionysios of Halicarnassos, *Roman Antiquities,* I, 12, 2.

winged wheels intended to facilitate his mission around the world. The back of the throne is decorated with the head of a griffin. Triptolemos holds in his hand a scepter as well as stalks of wheat which are marked by partially erased white painting. He turns around towards two women, the goddesses Demeter and Core/Persephone. While the difference between mother and daughter is not marked on the image by signs indicating any disparity in age, one could think that the first, with her two torches, is Persephone, while the second one on the left, because she holds a plow, is Demeter. The presence of the agricultural tool is rare in this type of scene (only two examples of it are known) but it highlights in a remarkable way the basic character of the episode. Demeter teaches man about tilling the soil and Triptolemos is going to give him the wheat. Through the presence of a technical instrument which might seem trivial is expressed an essential aspect of what seems to constitute the teaching given in the temple of Demeter in Eleusis at the time of the Mysteries which are "impossible to reveal."

Core, carried off by Hades, disappears below the earth; when finally restored to her mother, she comes back to the earth for a time, and vegetation grows once again. The cycle of germination is linked to the decision of Zeus, as the Homeric Hymn to Demeter recalls: "He

146. ATTIC RED-FIGURE KRATER, HEKTOR PAINTER
430 BC, HEIGHT 0.39 M
PARIS, CABINET DES MÉDAILLES, BIBLIOTHÈQUE NATIONALE

4. *Homeric Hymn to Demeter,* 464-5 and 471-2.

agreed that in the cycle of the year the girl would spend one third in the hazy darkness and the other two with you…Demeter immediately made fruitful plowing to grow the grain: the entire vast earth was burdened with leaves and flowers."[4]

On the krater by the Hektor painter the presence of the plow expressively shows the bond with the earth which seems essential to the Athenians; one sees it in the symbolic importance of the sacrifice, where meats and grains are closely joined in the relationship of men to gods; one also meets it in the claim of native origin which is based on the story of the birth of Erichthonios, who was born of the Earth.

Among the native Athenian heroes, Theseus occupies an essential place and is the object of numerous representations. More than 700 vases recall his exploits, of which nearly half are dedicated to the victory over the Minotaur, a struggle with a monster which links Theseus with Herakles.

Contrary to Erichthonios or Triptolemos, who are closely related to Attic soil, Theseus is a figure of uprooting. Because he could not have children, Aegeus the king of Athens went to consult the oracle at Delphi who answered him with an enigma: "Do not go to loosen the neck of the wineskin, oh great prince, before having reached Athens."[5] On the road home, Aegeus stopped at Troezen and told the king Pittheus what the god had said to him. The king understood that he must make Aegeus drink, and while he slept under his roof, he made his own daughter Aethra enter the bed of Aegeus. And so Theseus was born, son of Aegeus and Aethra, raised in Troezen by his grandfather. Others say that Theseus is the son of Poseidon who coupled with Aethra that same night. Although Theseus therefore has a two-fold origin, which might be either human or divine, it is certain that he was not born in Athens; as a child kept in secret, he had eventually to make himself known.

5. Plutarch, *The Life of Theseus,* 3, 5.

The myth of Theseus is a myth of the conquest of power and territory. The young man, advised by his mother, found in Troezen the weapons which his father had buried on his journey; thanks to these weapons he acquired an identity (much like Patroklos with the armor of Achilles). It was left to this bastard, this stranger, to make himself known in Athens. The first exploits of Theseus take place on the road from Troezen to Athens, all along the Isthmus of Corinth that was overrun with horrible bandits.

A cup in the museum in Florence evokes some of the exploits of this hero in the form of a cycle, with outstanding originality. The whole of the vase, interior and exterior, is dedicated to Theseus, who is shown naked like an ephebe or a young athlete. On one of the sides, three episodes are joined. To the left, facing Theseus, who is armed with an axe, a figure with an unkempt beard is hanging from a bent tree: it is the bandit Sinis, the "bender of pine trees," who had the habit of tearing apart the bodies of travelers by hanging them from branches drawn tight like a bow.

In the center, Theseus turns the bandit Sciron upside down, taking him by the feet, as Plutarch tells in his *Life of Theseus:* "He killed Sciron by throwing him down from high up on the rocks. According to the most widespread opinion, this bandit robbed passers-by; according to some others, he carried insolence and pride to the point of holding his feet out to strangers and asking them to wash them, and then, when they did, with a kick of his heel he pushed them into the sea."[6] The painter has drawn here an enormous rocky mass which is there not to describe the landscape but to define Sciron's way of working. On the ground in black silhouette one notices the large bronze basin used for washing the feet *(podanipter)*. It is in principle the mark of refined hospitality: one welcomes the traveler by washing his feet. But Sciron is a monster who radically inverts this behavior: he has his own feet washed, and by pushing him from the top of the cliff, kills the stranger, the *xenos,* who is in principle sacred according to the Greek rules of hospitality.

The same happens on the right of the image where this time Theseus graples with Procrustes. He, near Eleusis, had the habit of forcing travelers to stretch out on a bed and then to pull or cut off their limbs in order to adjust them to the size of it. The double axe which Theseus holds is that which the monster uses to torture his guests. Again the laws of the *xenia,* of Greek hospitality, are flouted. In his journey from Troezen to Athens, Theseus reestablishes order and the rules of society. Plutarch explains: "He punished the wicked by using against them the same type of violence that they would inflict upon others; he made them submit, as a just punishment, to the same forms of torture which they used unjustly."[7]

In this sense Theseus, who is often compared to Herakles, clearly sets himself apart. The trajectory of Theseus goes from the peripheral world towards the city of Athens, while Herakles moves away from Mycenae up to the limits of the earth. Theseus is a young man who reestablishes the social order and who, on becoming king, unites the territory of Attica; Herakles rids the world of hybrid monsters who, at its borders, threaten all of humanity. Herakles became a god, while Theseus is a political hero.

Nevertheless, the connections between Theseus, the hero of Athens, and Herakles the panhellenic hero, are not lacking. The first often

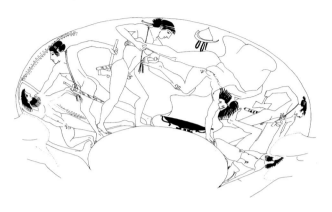

147. ATTIC RED-FIGURE CUP, DOKIMASIA PAINTER
480 BC, DIAMETER 0.27 M
FLORENCE, ARCHAEOLOGICAL MUSEUM

6. Plutarch. *Life of Theseus,* 10, 1.

7. *Ibid,* 11, 3

echoes the second, especially in the visual arts. Thus, the decoration of the temple of Hephaistos (in modern times sometimes incorrectly called the Theseion), on top of the Agora of Athens, associates the exploits of Theseus with those of Herakles, without doubt to give the local hero a status equal to that of the son of Zeus.

Similarly, on the cup in Florence, the second obverse plays upon this homology, in taking up again the episode of the bull of Marathon. In Crete, Herakles confronted a bull made furious by Poseidon; being able to overcome it, he brought it back to Argos, to his cousin Eurystheus who dedicated it to Hera. But the goddess, refusing such an offering because it came from Herakles, freed the animal, which, in crossing the isthmus, ravaged Attica. This is the same bull which Theseus in turn confronts on the plain of Marathon. The young naked hero succeeds in stopping the animal, which has fallen on its forequarters. He has passed a strap around the horns and feet of the beast which he also holds by the tail. The two women who frame the group emphasize by their frightened departure the valor of this exploit of Theseus.

According to certain versions, this bull, first from Crete and then from Marathon, would be the same one with which Pasiphae, the wife of Minos, king of Crete, fell in love. From this monstrous love, which Daedalus made possible by constructing a heifer inside which Pasiphae concealed herself and which the bull came to protect, was born an unnatural hybrid. The major exploit of Theseus, the one most often represented, is precisely the killing of the Minotaur. The scene figures on the medallion of the cup in Florence. Theseus is this time dressed in a short tunic *(chiton)*. It is no longer the still unknown ephebe, but the hero who leads the procession of the young people of Athens who are delivered from the ferocity of the Minotaur.

King Minos, the conqueror of the Athenians, had imposed upon them a heavy tribute: every nine years, seven young boys and seven young girls, chosen in a lottery, were to be delivered to the monster. "The most tragic account shows the children carried off to Crete, killed in the labyrinth by the Minotaur, or even dying there after having wandered around trying to find a way out." Theseus, recognized by his father in Athens, "thought it just that he share in the fate of his fellow citizens; and so he offered himself voluntarily, without participating in the lottery, and he led the expedition." [8]

Guided by Ariadne, the daughter of Minos, Theseus entered the

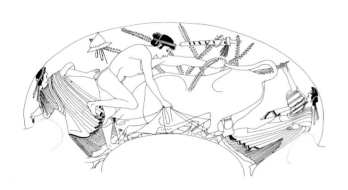

148. ATTIC RED-FIGURE CUP, DOKIMASIA PAINTER
480 BC, DIAMETER 0.27 M
FLORENCE, ARCHAEOLOGICAL MUSEUM

▶ **149.** INTERIOR OF THE CUP, FIGURES 147, 148

8. Ibid, 17, 2

labyrinth which was constructed by Daedalus and killed the monster. On the medallion of the cup, a man with the head of a bull falls to the ground between two rocks. Theseus has seized him by one of his horns and with his sword he cuts his throat, which bleeds profusely. The cap of the hero, suspended in the background, here and also on the other side of the vase, indicates that he is a traveler, not a warrior.

The choice of exploits grouped in this way on this cup forms a sort of journey across the isthmus, from Troezen to Athens; then in Attica, and to Marathon; and finally in Crete where Theseus, the son of King Aegeus, legitimizes his place as royal heir through his heroic devotion. The juxtaposition of scenes in the form of a cycle clearly indicates that which characterizes Theseus: the series of tests is as much a trajectory in space, inscribed in the geography of the Greek world, as a journey of initiation in which he moves from anonymous illegitimacy to the status of the future king of Athens. Step by step the royal and political dimension of Theseus is affirmed. This cyclical organization – of which there are few examples in Attic vase-painting – seems to have been chosen by the cup painters in order to make more clearly perceptible and to make visually real this transformation of the Athenian hero.

In the archaic period, only the episode of the Minotaur was of interest to the painters, as on an amphora in the Louvre, where the hero has nothing of the fragility of the ephebe: bearded, powerfully planted on his legs, he holds the Minotaur by the neck and slits his throat with his sword. Blood runs out in torrents. Between the legs of Theseus flies a bird, without doubt a good omen. On each side two pairs of young people, girls and boys, frame the scene, admiring the deed which sets them free, while on the other side of the same vase Herakles confronts the Nemean lion.

◄ 150. ATTIC BLACK-FIGURE AMPHORA, GROUP OF LONDON B 174
540 BC, HEIGHT 0.42 M
PARIS, LOUVRE

We have seen on the neck of the François vase how Theseus leads the young people of Athens. At the head of the procession, on the right, he stands before the wet-nurse *(trophos)* and Ariadne; she holds out to him a ball of yarn, the guiding thread which leads him out of the labyrinth. Behind Theseus, seven young girls alternate with six young boys holding hands in a continuous chain. The lyre which Theseus holds makes him the chorus master; it suggests a dance, perhaps the one whose invention we attribute to him, on the way home towards Athens, in Delos – the *geranos,* the dance of the crane. One will note above all that Theseus, contrary to Herakles, appears here as the

151. ATTIC BLACK-FIGURE KRATER, DETAIL OF NECK, KLEITIAS
570 BC, HEIGHT 0.66 M
FLORENCE, ARCHAEOLOGICAL MUSEUM

▶ **152.** ATTIC RED-FIGURE KRATER, SYRISKOS PAINTER
480 BC, HEIGHT 0.41 M
PARIS, CABINET DES MÉDAILLES, BIBLIOTHÈQUE NATIONALE

9. Bacchylides, *Dithyrambs,* III, 36-37 and 56-57.

10. Plutarch, *The Life of Theseus,* 35, 8.

envoy of a community, at the head of a group of young people chosen in a lottery who are in a way the product of the city of Athens, whose safety he secures before becoming its king, finally recognized by his own people as the successor of Aegeus.

This legitimization of the bastard, this need for recognition, is an essential characteristic of the figure of Theseus, which we find again in another episode, this time more rare: that of the dive to the bottom of the sea. At the time of the Cretan expedition, Theseus, in front of Minos, the son of Zeus, claims his divine origin: he calls himself the son of Poseidon. Minos then issues a challenge, and throws a ring into the waves: "Bring back from the bottom of the sea this brilliant jewel of gold which decorates my hand. Boldly cast your body down into the home of your father." And as Bacchylides tells it, "the dolphins living in the sea quickly brought the great Theseus to the home of his father. He came to the palace of the gods." [9]

On a krater by the Syriskos painter, Poseidon sits on a throne at the center of the image, trident in hand, feet resting on a support decorated with tiny dolphins. The young Theseus extends his right hand to his divine father; their gesture of alliance marks the recognition and the harmony which guarantees the triumph of Theseus. Behind the god, standing, a woman – probably Amphitrite – holds a crown intended for the hero. And so Poseidon, the unfortunate rival of Athena, ensures the victory of the most political of all the heroes of Attica.

The end of Theseus, which was not at all glorious, does not give rise to any particular iconography. He died in exile in Scyros and it was not until the 5th century BC that his glory was reborn in Athens. "At the battle of Marathon against the Medes, many soldiers believed that they saw the ghost of Theseus in armor rushing forward at the front against the barbarians." [10] After the Persian wars, around 475 BC, the political leader Cimon searched for the bones of Theseus, at the order of the oracle at Delphi, and brought them back for burial in the center of the city.

The red-figure painters at the beginning of the 5th century BC

broadened the repertoire outside the episode of the Minotaur, creating cycles or retaining exploits that were until then poorly represented, until the moment when, in the city of Athens, the architects of the Hephaisteion put Theseus and Herakles close together in the decoration of the temple.

In these few examples one sees how, in the city, in an echo of the panhellenic figure of Herakles, a national legend which made Theseus the Athenian hero *par excellence* was constructed, the same one to whom Plutarch dedicated the first of his *Parallel Lives,* next to Romulus, the first of the Romans.

One cannot enter into detail in all the stories which constitute the mythic history of Athens. But it is still necessary to highlight two complementary aspects of this mythical elaboration: the proliferation of local legends and their implications for the political geography of classical Athens as well as, conversely, the recovery by the Attic repertoire of non-Athenian legends.

In Greece, the landscape is full of stories. A great many particular places, rivers, caves, trees, and rocks are connected to the stories of which the painters sometimes become the echo. At the beginning of the dialogue which bears his name, Phaedrus, in the company of Socrates, walks along the banks of the river Illissos. Coming to a tall plane tree, he asks: "Tell me, Socrates, isn't it from somewhere around here that they say Boreas carried off Orithyia? – Yes, that is what they say." [11]

On a pelike from approximately 440 BC, we see Boreas, the north wind. Winged and bearded, he jumps with arms extended, without touching the earth, towards a young girl who, on the other side of the vase, seems to innocently play ball. Oreithyia is the daughter of Erichthonios, the native-born king of primeval Athens. Boreas lives in Thrace. This scene of pursuit, true to a frequent pattern in which the gods carry off young girls (we remember Hades carrying off Persephone), marks the alliance between the god from the north and the Athenians. Pausanias explains: "Boreas...because of the ties of kinship which he had, came to the help of the Athenians in destroying the major part of the barbarian ships," [12] and Socrates recalls that near the Illissos there is an altar to Boreas, without doubt erected after the victory of Salamis.

And so the image, with a great economy of means, evokes a scene of pursuit which is not without historical and religious implications for

153, 154. ATTIC RED-FIGURE PELIKE. NOT ATTRIBUTED
440 BC. HEIGHT 0.17 M
PARIS. CABINET DES MÉDAILLES. BIBLIOTHÈQUE NATIONALE

11. Plato, *Phaedrus,* 229b.
12. Pausanias I, 19, 5.

the local culture of Attica. Often the detail of such representations escapes the modern viewer, because it is not always possible for us to reconstruct, behind the image, the mythic, historic and topographic background which informs them.

Besides the local legends, one also meets in Attic imagery themes which belong to other cities, but of which Athens partially claims the prestige. This is the case of the Theban hero Oedipus, of whose misfortunes we know. The mistaken old blind man, feeling that his end is near, seeks refuge in Attica, at Colonus, where Theseus greets him and protects him from the claims of his hostile sons. In one of his last tragedies, *Oedipus at Colonus,* performed around 405 BC, Sophocles portrays these final moments of the fallen king, whose tomb remains hidden in Attica.

The Achilles painter, forty years earlier, retained another aspect of this legend, which was not the end of Oedipus but his beginning. On an amphora with twisted handles, a man advances, hat at his neck and lance in his hand; he carries a child in his arms. The pair is isolated on a background of black glaze, with no frame or ornament other than a line on the ground. Only two parallel inscriptions give their full meaning to this scene. The adult is named *Euphorbos* and the child *Oidipous*. It is rare for a man to carry a child; it is normally the concern of women. This apparently peaceful scene refers to the first misfortune of Oedipus. The shepherd Euphorbos received the task of abandoning the child, of exposing him to wild animals; he is shown here on his way to accomplish his evil task. The Achilles painter often proceeded in this manner, isolating a figure without dramatizing the event to which it refers. The image remains implicit; it tells nothing, but suggests to the viewer an entire mythic ensemble which his memory already knows.

Thebes, seen from Athens, is overcome by misfortune; the child Oedipus, quietly nestled in the arms of Euphorbos, does not know where he is brought, but the Athenian of the 5th century BC knows that Oedipus will end his days in Colonus where he finally rests thanks to the protection of Theseus.

Many of these vase paintings, conveying stories which are echoed by the poetry of the past, allow the Athenian drinkers who are gathered at the banquet not only to make real and current and to transmit their mythical values, but above all to define their own individual as well as civic and political identity.

155, 156. ATTIC RED-FIGURE AMPHORA, ACHILLES PAINTER
450 BC, HEIGHT 0.49 M
PARIS, CABINET DES MÉDAILLES, BIBLIOTHÈQUE NATIONALE

DIONYSOS AND HIS FOLLOWERS 9

▶ 157. ATTIC RED-FIGURE AMPHORA, KLEOPHRADES PAINTER
500 BC, HEIGHT 0.56 M
MUNICH, ANTIKENSAMMLUNG

158. ATTIC BLACK-FIGURE AMPHORA, DIOSPHOS PAINTER
500-490 BC, HEIGHT 0.25 M
PARIS, CABINET DES MÉDAILLES, BIBLIOTHÈQUE NATIONALE

Of all the gods of the Greek pantheon, Dionysos is certainly the one most often depicted on wine vases. There is nothing surprising in this: he is at home at the banquet. Nevertheless, we must put this into perspective: Greek polytheism does not give him a major role in the forms of worship or in the sanctuaries. In Attic ceramics, the representations of this son of Zeus and Semele are countless, as if each painter had wanted to give his own version of it. Here, more than ever, it is necessary to limit ourselves to a few major characteristics.

The essential traits of Dionysos are put in place very early in Attic imagery; one finds almost all of them brought together on an amphora attributed to the Kleophrades painter, on which the god moves forward while turning around in the middle of his procession. His long wavy locks spread out on his shoulders and his beard is bushy. In the 5th century BC, Dionysos wears this kind of a beard; he only becomes an unbearded adolescent over time, towards the end of the century. Here he is a vigorous adult; he wears on his shoulders a panther skin whose paws are tied around his neck; his long chiton and many-pleated cloak give him a feminine manner which belies his beard. Crowned with ivy, he holds a vine whose foliage forms a sort of nimbus: these two quasi-tentacled plants indicate the vegetable energy which characterizes the god, just like the vase that he holds in his hand, the kantharos with high vertical handles, an attribute of Dionysos and Herakles.

Feminized, animalized, and plant-like, Dionysos is in motion; he comes from elsewhere, he is the other, even within the city of Athens. Just like Athena, the daughter of Zeus alone, Dionysos had to come into the world, something which did not happen without pain. This son of Zeus had a Theban princess, Semele, for his mother; also a Theban princess was Alcmene, the mother of Heracles. But Semele could not carry Dionysos to term. The jealous Hera then gave deadly advice to Semele: to demand of Zeus that he show himself to her in all his power. The ruler of Olympus resisted, but he was bound by an oath; when he appeared to Semele, she was immediately struck by lightning. Zeus took in the child that she was carrying, and sewed him up in his thigh.

On a small black-figure amphora we see Zeus seated, holding a scepter and a thunderbolt. In front of him, Hera turns around to look at the child who stands upright on the thighs of Zeus. An already-formed adolescent, he waves two lit torches. An inscription names him *kalos Diosphos*. While the term *kalos,* beautiful, is easy to understand, the name *Diosphos* (from

which comes the name given to this painter) is less obvious. We interpret it as *Dios phos,* "the man of Zeus," rather than "light of Zeus" (suggested by the presence of the torches). The term *phos,* according to the way the word is accented, can have either meaning. We meet here a variation of the name *Dio nysos,* "son of Zeus," in a scene which shows birth by the male, under the gaze of Hera, the jealous wife of Zeus.

Different from Athena who was born completely armed and already an adult, the child Dionysos had to grow up in hiding in order to escape the wrath of Hera. This period of childhood gives Dionysos a biographical dimension which makes him one of the most human of gods.

On a hydria by the Syleus painter, Zeus in person (he is named by an inscription) presents the child to two women who greet him: one, seated near a column, touches him with her right hand and holds in her left a branch of ivy which corresponds, like a kind of hyphen, to the one held by the small Dionysos. To the right another woman, crowned with ivy and scepter in hand, turns around, motionless. The solemn aspect of these two figures, which is not due exclusively to the style of the painter, but also to the presence of the column – which implies a constructed space, a house or a palace – suggests that these women are not maenads; nor are they simple nymphs – who live in uncivilized spaces – but perhaps royal figures, such as Ino, the wife of Athamas, the king of Orchomenos, to whom Dionysos is sometimes entrusted. Beneath an apparent calm a violent tragedy is suggested. The jealous Hera drives Ino mad, making her kill her own children.

Many stories are connected to the difficult beginnings of Dionysos, to his secret childhood, his own madness (inflicted by Hera), and his wanderings to India and Asia, before his return to Greece, and to Thebes in particular. The painters sometimes depicted such episodes, especially in the 5th century BC, in red-figures, at a time when the tragic poets presented the same stories.

In black-figure painting, the repertoire confines itself to a more general vision of Dionysos, which on drinking vases makes him the god of wine and the feast, close to the men with whom he is sometimes confused. Such is the case with a cup of imposing dimensions, more than 40 cm (16 inches) in diameter, whose decoration is entirely dedicated to Dionysos. On the exterior, the god, accompanied by a maenad who dances to the sound of rattles and gesticulating satyrs, prepares to leave in a chariot.

159. ATTIC RED-FIGURE HYDRIA, SYLEUS PAINTER
480 BC, HEIGHT 0.38 M
PARIS, CABINET DES MÉDAILLES, BIBLIOTHÈQUE NATIONALE

The bodies of the satyrs are speckled like the coat of an animal. One of
them, behind the team of horses, turns his face towards the viewer; with
arm raised, he salutes, and his bent head, which has the appearance of a
mask with its wide-eyed stare, seems to invite the drinker to follow the
procession. On the inside of the cup, around a white ground medallion
on which a grimacing Gorgon stands out, a whole troupe of satyrs and
maenads move about underneath a vine. The branches, carved out at the
top, run all around the entire bowl, starting with the two intertwined
stalks which are level with the ears of the *gorgoneion*. In the upper part,
grapes are harvested under the control of Dionysos, who is seated on a
mule; the satyrs fill tall wicker baskets which stand on the ground as well
as a large basin which is more flat. One of them carries a basket on his
back, in the direction of the press, which is directly below the beard of
the Gorgon. Great activity is the rule: a satyr crushes the grapes in a tray
from which the juice runs into a jar over which a maenad steps. Under
the press creeps another satyr as if to drink from the stream of wine,
while to the left one of his fellow creatures climbs up a vine.

160. ATTIC RED-FIGURE CUP, NOT ATTRIBUTED
520 BC, MAXIMUM DIAMETER 0.43 M
PARIS, CABINET DES MÉDAILLES, BIBLIOTHÈQUE NATIONALE

161. INTERIOR OF THE CUP, FIGURE 160

▶▶ 162. DETAIL OF THE INTERIOR OF THE CUP, FIGURE 160

163. DETAIL OF THE CUP, FIGURE I

164. ATTIC RED-FIGURE CUP, BRYGOS PAINTER
490 BC, MAXIMUM DIAMETER 0.36 M
PARIS, CABINET DES MÉDAILLES, BIBLIOTHÈQUE NATIONALE

▶ 165. INTERIOR OF THE CUP, FIGURE 164

There is nothing in this harvest that would resemble hard work. The painter does not try to describe human toil, but to develop around Dionysos a festive circle of joyful satyrs. The inside of this large cup, which is more decorative than functional, is entirely filled with branches and bunches of grapes, the come-and-go of satyrs and maenads in the process of preparing the wine, which will be drunk from this very cup.

A gift from Dionysos to men, wine must be mastered and controlled, as much in its making as in its consumption. On the François vase, Dionysos brings Hephaistos back to Olympus and leads a procession of satyrs in which wine, music, and sexuality are explicitly joined. These same elements are tirelessly taken up again in the imagery on vases from the 6th and 5th centuries, through a whole play of variations.

The Brygos painter is one of those who knew how to create some of these most remarkable variations. On the medallion of a cup appears an exceptional Dionysos-as-musician. The instrument which the god uses is typical of the *comos;* it is a sort of lyre with long uprights, a *barbiton,* which often accompanied lyric poetry. Here Dionysos, with his plectrum in hand, sings with his head thrown back and his beard pointing towards the sky, in a posture that is very human and one rarely taken by the god himself. Around him dance two satyrs giving rhythm to their movements with the sound of rattles. One of them holds a vine branch which overruns the background of the image; the other is dressed in a panther skin which flutters on his back and amplifies his movement.

On the outside, the same Dionysos, with kantharos and vine branch in hand, walks next to an ass which raises its tail and seems to bray, while the satyr who follows him sings to the sound of the *barbiton.* He is dressed in a panther skin and wears flapped boots like the Thracian horsemen. The tail of the ass crosses his chest and becomes confused with his own, as well as with the panther skin. A maenad follows, with hair undone, and brandishing a *thyrsus* – a long staff with a pine cone or a bunch of ivy at the top – and a serpent which is wrapped around her left arm. She is dressed in a long pleated chiton and a spotted fawn pelt. At the head of the procession a second satyr carries a wineskin on his shoulder and lifts a panther by its tail. This familiarity with wild animals characterizes the Dionysian world. The hides of fawns *(nebrides)* or of panthers *(pardalides)* indicate a certain kind of savagery and make animals of the maenads, while they accentuate the animal nature of the satyrs which is already inscribed in their anatomy.

Wine, music, and dance appear once again, but on an imaginary plane, and no longer, as with the images of the banquet, in the way of men who see themselves in the mirrors of vases. With Dionysos there in person one moves in a fantasy world where the limits imposed upon humans are abolished.

The god is often shown with all or part of his retinue. The Amasis painter, on an amphora which represents on one side the meeting between Athena and Poseidon, has shown only maenads on the reverse. There are two of them, dancing at the same step, taking each other by the shoulders in front of the god holding a kantharos who greets them. Both hold long branches of ivy which frame them, as well as live game: a hare held at the end of one arm, and a small deer held against the body of the maenad in the foreground. In addition, she wears the skin of a panther whose head hangs to her knees. The minuteness of the incisions, the colorful embellishments and the outline used for rendering female flesh (rather than the usual white paint) are all characteristic of this painter-potter whose signature *Amasis epoiesen* runs along the top of the image.

In red-figure painting, the representation of satyrs is enriched by numerous vivid details which renew the simple repetition of the archaic procession. On a plate signed *Epictetos egraphsen,* already mentioned in terms of the banquet, appears a satyr with an *aulos.* We have seen the difference between the man who carries his flute holster on his shoulder (fig. 14) and the satyr who hangs it from his penis. The elegance of the design tones down the obscenity of the motif and the implicit wordplay between *subene,* the name of the holster and *su binein,* "fuck you."

The satyrs are often obscene and grotesque, always agitated and gesticulating. Thus, on the medallion of a cup, one of them dances with thighs spread apart and hands on his hips in front of a banqueter whose raised knee hides the satyr's pelvic area. This recumbent figure, crowned with ivy, extends a phiale, the vase for libations. The company of the satyr and the presence of the ritual vase make this drinker more than a man: he is Dionysos in the flesh, feasting in the manner of humans.

The obverse of this cup also transposes the model of the human *symposion* into the domain of Dionysian fantasy. Recumbent not on cushions but on rocks, as if for a rural festival, a naked woman, crowned with ivy and with rattles in hand, keeps company with two banqueting satyrs. The woman resembles more the courtesans of a *symposion* attended by men than the maenads of a Dionysian procession. Moreover, the reference to the banquet is repeated by the

167. ATTIC RED-FIGURE PLATE, SIGNED EPICTETOS
510 BC, DIAMETER 0.19 M
PARIS, CABINET DES MÉDAILLES, BIBLIOTHÈQUE NATIONALE

168. ATTIC RED-FIGURE CUP, COLMAR PAINTER
490 BC, DIAMETER 0.33 M
FLORENCE, ARCHAEOLOGICAL MUSEUM

1. Euripides, *Bacchae*, 677-774.

▶ **170.** ATTIC RED-FIGURE CUP, MACRON
490 BC, MAXIMUM DIAMETER 0.42 M
PARIS, LOUVRE

171. ATTIC RED-FIGURE CUP, MACRON
490 BC, MAXIMUM DIAMETER 0.33 M
MUNICH, ANTIKENSAMMLUNG

ornamental motif which runs below the scene: a series of objects in silhouette sending us back to the *symposion* (fig. 17 and 136).

The relationships between satyrs and maenads outside the presence of Dionysos is the object of many representations. In black-figure on the François vase for example, they form pairs of partners always ready to couple. In red-figure, around the year 500 BC, it seems these relationships change. The maenads do not always let themselves be persuaded; the trance, the *mania*, to which they owe their name *(mainades),* and which often seized them as we have seen on the cup by the Brygos painter, is essentially the result of music and dance, without any use of wine or sexuality. Such a distinction is explicit in the *Bacchae* of Euripides,[1] where it is man who imagines such orgies of wine and sex, while the testimony of the shepherd who has seen them indicates clearly that it is not so.

The maenads do not always submit to the satyrs, whose lewdness is more and more often unavailing. One can compare two cups attributed to the same painter, Macron. On one cup the maenad, who holds a *thyrsus* in one hand and a panther in the other, has put her arm around the shoulder of a satyr who holds her by the neck and slides a furtive hand underneath her pleated chiton. On the other cup, however, the maenad who is crowned with ivy and wears a panther skin around her shoulders draws back with arm raised, away from a satyr who tries to touch her and whom she pushes back with her leveled *thyrsus*.

The Kleophrades painter proposes an entirely different version of these relationships on a hydria preserved in Rouen. The maenad is asleep with her eyes closed and her head resting on a rock, the *thyrsus* across her body. Curious, a satyr leaning over her lifts her dress and slips his hand between her thighs. She sees nothing and does not move. To the left another satyr, on his knees and leaning on his hands with fingers curled, seems with astonishment to discover his own virility. Here the wide-eyed satyrs are dawdling in curiosity and lechery, but the maenad, quietly dozing, remains outside these desires. The satyr makes himself a voyeur and the image in turn makes the viewer of the vase a voyeur and a witness to the lewdness of the satyrs and the beauty of the feminine body. This latter aspect is emphasized by the inscription *kalos* at the top of the painting, which echoes this beauty.

There is something naïve and sometimes childish about the satyrs. They are like young animals let loose and out of control, whose

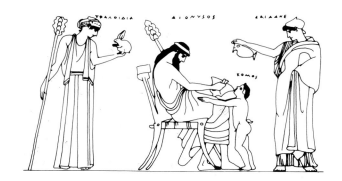

◀◀ **172.** ATTIC RED-FIGURE HYDRIA, KLEOPHRADES PAINTER
500 BC, HEIGHT 0.34 M
ROUEN, ARCHAEOLOGICAL MUSEUM

173, 174. ATTIC RED-FIGURE KRATER, POLYGNOTOS GROUP
430 BC, HEIGHT 0.23 M
COMPIÈGNE, MUSÉE VIVENEL

gesticulation causes laughter. The painters of the 5th century BC exploited this aspect in developing the figure of the child satyr, the young unbearded satyr discovering the world around him. On a krater from around 430 BC, one witnesses the education of one of these youths. It is no longer an adolescent Dionysos among the maenads or nymphs, but on the contrary the adult god who educates a small satyr by letting him drink from his kantharos. The inscriptions which accompany the scene are very illuminating. The seated bearded god is of course named Dionysos; but his young partner is named *Komos,* the festival of drinkers; a programmatic name for sure. As for the women who surround them, the one who pours the wine is Ariadne, the companion of Dionysos; the other who holds out a hare, the play companion of the satyr, is named *Tragodia,* "Tragedy." We are thus returned to the genre of theatre of which Dionysos is the master, since it was at the Dionysia, during the festivals in his honor, that dramatic contests took place. The image here describes none of the representations in their scenic reality. The presence of this feminine figure, which we could call allegorical, is enough to evoke another domain reserved for Dionysos. Wine and theatre are two essential dimensions of the Athenian worship of Dionysos.

The festivals in honor of this god are numerous. The details partially escape us and the images do not allow us to recreate their unfolding.

They content themselves with suggesting certain aspects of it, by means of a name or a presence, which the ancient viewer would know well. A cup from around 540 BC gives us a good example, with variations from one side to the other. The scene represents on one side a group of six men in the process of raising a sort of platform upon which rises a long slanting pole ending in a tassel provided with an eye. A fat pot-bellied standing man keeps this immense *phallos* erect, and at the top of it is attached a strip of cloth. The man holds in his other hand a branch of ivy, a Dionysian symbol which becomes explicit on the other side.

The bearers are eight in number and almost all have an erection; with legs bent, seven of them raise the platform facing an eighth man at the front, who buttresses it from the other direction; the front of this structure is decorated with a tassel similar to that which tops the pole itself. This pole, identical to the one on the other side, is held this time by an immense satyr, who leans forward with his backside in the air, and is himself mounted by a miniature man who lifts a large drinking horn. Various ropes on both sides seem to assure the maneuvering of this strange machine, which seems made to be raised in stages.

One can recognize here a scene of phallophory, of the transport of the *phallos* in honor of Dionysos, a festival for which there exist parallel examples, in Delos for instance, where we find an inscription which sets out its preparations. But here the image, in varying the details from one side to the other, in modifying the scale of the figures, and in introducing an out-sized satyr, accentuates the symbolic effectiveness of the festival to the detriment of its realistic description. The ivy, the drinking horn, and the *phallos* convey the power of Dionysos, the god of wine and of vegetation which is always green, and of the most unbridled sexuality. Dionysos himself never has an erection – he is never ithyphallic – as such obscene behavior is reserved only for satyrs. On this cup the satyr and the pot-bellied, grotesque man lead the procession of the *phallos* in honor of Dionysos. The male genitalia becomes an autonomous object, carried by the male collectivity; detached from the bodies of those who accompany it, it occupies a central place in the Dionysian festival.

The drinking vase, whose decoration plays at varying the points of view of the ritual and the phallic procession, sends us back outside the restrained space of the *symposion* to other moments and to other festivals whose details escape us, but which tie the presence of Dionysos to the city of Athens, and make him a dominant character in its figurative repertoire.

175, 176. ATTIC BLACK-FIGURE CUP, NOT ATTRIBUTED
540 BC
FLORENCE, ARCHAEOLOGICAL MUSEUM

EPILOGUE

▶ 177. ATTIC RED-FIGURE KRATER PRONOMOS PAINTER
410 BC, HEIGHT 0.75 M
NAPLES, ARCHAEOLOGICAL MUSEUM

1. All the names in italics correspond
to the inscriptions on the vase.

With time, Dionysos grows younger. At the end of the 5th century, he loses his beard and the painters make him a seductive young man. This is how he appeared in the company of Ariadne on the upper register of a volute-krater from around 410 BC which serves not to end our discussion but to bring us a last look at Athenian vases.

The principal scene is organized on two levels which complement each other, conforming to the practice of painters of that time. The surface of the krater is no longer well-ordered and divided into clearly separate zones, each treating distinct subjects, as on the François vase, but is on the contrary entirely occupied by a scene whose characters are set out in tiered rows on a double register. Many of these actors are gathered around *Dionysos,*[1] who is leaning on a couch similar to the beds at a banquet, but turned in the opposite direction, with his head on the left. To the left of the bed a bearded man holds a mask in his hand; he is dressed like a king, but there is no inscription to name him. At the foot of the bed accompanied by *Himeros,* Desire, with wings spread, a woman is seated, and in her hand is the mask of a queen. The detail is noteworthy: the actor who plays the feminine role is unmasked; but the painter makes this actor a woman, which is contrary to the Greek practice which requires that all roles be played by men. This is the first indication which reminds us that this image does not reproduce that which is real, but plays with the categories which it represents. Further to the right, a standing man who wears a breastplate and has a club and a lionskin on his shoulder holds a mask whose face is set within the jaws of a lion: he is *Herakles,* which is confirmed by the inscription near his club. There are, then, around the bed of Dionysus three principal actors, all unmasked, of which only one, Herakles, is named.

Facing Herakles is a man in a hairy costume with a panther skin on his shoulder, who raises the mask of a hoary satyr: he is Silenus, the

chorus master of the satyrs. In effect, one notices on each side of this central group of actors a series of clean-shaven young men who are naked and who wear at their waists short pants of animal skin furnished with a discretely erect penis and a horse's tail. Almost all hold in their hands a bearded mask with pointed ears, which is the mask of the satyr. These young people therefore form a chorus of satyrs. On the top, one counts three on the left and one on the right; below, four on the right and two on the left, plus a third who dances with left leg raised and arm extended. In total, there are eleven young people led by Silenus.

In the central axis of the vase, just below the bed of Dionysos, an *aulos* player sits on a chair; his name is inscribed: *Pronomos* – the celebrated Theban musician whose existence is historically attested. Before him stands another musician with a lyre in his hand, *Charinos.* To the left of the satyr who dances is the poet *Demetrios,* who is seated on a table with a scroll in his hand, and next to whom is a lyre.

Therefore, all the parts of the image taken together put Dionysos, the god of the theater, and all his troupe, on display: the actors, and the chorus, as well as the author of the play, Demetrios, who holds his text in his hand, and the musicians who accompany the sung parts. The nature of the chorus defines the genre to which the play belongs: the satyr-play, which usually follows the tragic trilogy and which is written by the authors of the tragedies. This is the case, for example, with *The Cyclops* by Euripides, of which the protagonists, Odysseus and the Cyclops, are serious characters, but of which the chorus is composed of ludicrous satyrs.

On this krater, which is named after the musician who appears on it, Pronomos, the painter did not try to reproduce the theatrical action or to name the play. One certainly sees that the protagonists are a king and a queen, and that Herakles plays a role, but nothing allows us to identify the subject in a more precise way. If this can seem frustrating to the modern viewer, it is clear that for the painter and the viewers around the year 410 BC the question did not arise. They knew very well which play of Demetrios won the contest at the festivals in honor of Dionysos.

What the painter shows here is not the spectacle seen at the theatre, but the entire troupe, like a sort of didascalia, a sort of credit title which commemorates a victory. The tripods which frame the scene are in fact consecrated to Dionysos by those who are triumphant; the one on the right, placed on a column standing on a tiered pedestal, takes on a

178. FULL VIEW OF THE KRATER, FIGURE 177

monumental aspect which underlines this dimension of the image: victorious consecration in honor of Dionysos. The actors are not performing but are completely relaxed and unmasked, with one exception: the satyr who dances to the sound of the *aulos* played by Pronomos. He is in action and he wears his mask, which suddenly is no longer conspicuous as a thing of artifice: the dancer as he is pictured has the head of a satyr. His right foot extends beyond the decorative border which forms the ground, as if, by means of movement, the satyr were exiting the frame of the image. A vine which reaches Dionysos grows above his head on the axis which extends from his body, and it gives the dancer a direct connection to the god.

The painter has explored in a very subtle manner, through the play of masks which are held, raised or carried, the presentation of theatrical illusion. All the characters retain their costumes, but have stopped acting while they remove their masks. This pause in the action on stage puts us elsewhere. We do not see the scene, but the troupe. At the same time Dionysos is present among these characters, like a guest among his own people.

A further detail: the inscriptions which accompany these figures name them in various ways. The actor dressed as Herakles is named *Herakles,* which very clearly indicates his role. Whereas the satyrs – or rather the young people dressed as satyrs – are almost all accompanied by inscriptions which give their names as citizens: *Eunikos, Dorotheos, Euagon* on top at the left, *Kallias* on the right; *Nikomachos, Chairias* at the bottom on the left, *Dion* and *Philinos* on the right. Even the dancing satyr bears his name as a citizen, *Nikoleos.* And so, in the city, one's real identity and one's role in the play come together. Herakles is already unmasked and *Nikoleos* is still a satyr.

The image on the vase shapes the idea of the presentation. The theater is a form of visual experience where the citizen spectator sees — this is the meaning of the word theater — the heroes of the past as if they were present in front of him. This theatrical illusion is placed by the Athenians under the sign of Dionysos, in honor of whom they put on the play. The image of the Pronomos krater does not reconstruct this illusion, it goes beyond it: on one side it brings the satyrs of the play back to their nature as citizens, but at the same time it also places the god and his company in the middle of the victorious troupe. It is a shared presence which makes the favor of the god visible.

The votive tripods placed under the handles of the krater make it a commemorative piece, perhaps ordered by those in the chorus to celebrate their own victory at a private banquet. As it singles out each one of them, the vase recalls the public inscriptions engraved in honor of the victors at the dramatic contests. But while the inscriptions place the references to Dionysos, to the theatre and to the victorious citizens in a hierarchy, by clearly separating them, the krater produces a sort of interpenetration and osmosis of these different registers, in passing from one plane to another on the interior of the same image.

One finds on the other side of the vase a familiar scene of the Dionysian *comos.* The young god comes forward with lyre in hand and supported by a maenad. Eros in flight accompanies them while playing the cymbals. The couple is surrounded by dancing satyrs and maenads who carry thyrsoi and torches. At the junction of this side of the vase and the main scene on the other side, two satyrs are found back to back; one of them, on the left, is unmasked, and the mask which he holds behind his back is turned towards the dancing satyr who participates in the Dionysian *comos.* In bringing them together in this way, the painter makes explicit the workings of an image which can show us the reality of the theatre as well as place before the eyes of the viewer the divine procession of which the mythical reality is made here purely pictorial. The power of illusion works on the double register of the scene and of the image; the game of what is real and of appearance, of the *phantasia,* the imaginary quality of which the painters of Athens explored and developed the richness.

Between the François vase and the Pronomos vase, the two kraters which have marked our journey from beginning to end, a whole range of graphic invention has been displayed, against which we understand Plato would have been on guard.

APPENDICES

Greek vases are a relatively recent discovery in the panorama of classic archaeology. Unlike various monuments, statues, coins and inscriptions known since the Renaissance, the vases became part of the knowledge of archaeologists only belatedly. While certain isolated pieces of pottery could have been seen by Pollaiuolo, for example, in the 15th century, it is not until the 18th century that this class of objects, still poorly identified, imposed itself upon the attention of scholars.

At this time, around 1760, access to Greece, which was still under Ottoman rule, was difficult for Europeans. There existed some collections of vases, discovered for the most part in Southern Italy or in Etruria, and considered Etruscan. One finds them in certain cabinets of curiosities – eccentric assemblies of archaeological objects and natural wonders – more often as ornaments at the tops of book cases than as objects of systematic study.

Towards the middle of the 18th century, tastes changed and curiosity was stimulated. Scholars such as the Count de Caylus sought to understand the technique of creating the vases, as well as interpreting the figures seen upon them. He was one of the first to place importance upon the direct study of the objects, which he published in his *Recueil d'Antiquités*, especially the vases which he then gave to the king and which are today in the Cabinet des Médailles. Sir William Hamilton, the special envoy of the King of England at the court of Naples, was fascinated with Greek vases upon his arrival in Campania. He quick-

ly formed a top-quality collection, the publication of which he entrusted to the knight Pierre Hughes d'Hancarville, an inventive and slightly crooked scholar. This first catalogue of vases, a series of four sumptuous folios filled with watercolor prints, was a masterpiece of publishing at the time, if not a model of science. In 1762 this collection was sold as a whole to the British Museum, which as a result became for a long time the foremost great European museum to own a good collection of vases.

And so the fashion began; the factory of Mr. Wedgwood, which he called "Etruria", was inspired by these vases and by their publication to offer them in modern equivalents. One of the very first examples, before 1789, imitated the form of a calyx krater and used as decoration not a vase image but a carved stone motif, drawn from the collection of Caylus. Ceramics and carving merged to feed the neoclassical taste.

Interest began with aristocrats, collectors and those who inspired fashion, rather than with the scholars who pioneered a new discipline: besides epigraphy and numismatics, now ceramics. A German scholar even coined the term angeiology, the science of vases.

The decisive impetus was given, however, a few decades later, following the extraordinary finds made in the necropolis of Vulci, about a hundred kilometers north of Rome. As is often the case, it was an accident which led to the discovery; an ox pulling a plow was swallowed up in the collapse of a tomb chamber. These underground dwelling places,

often decorated with frescoes, contained, when they were still intact, many vases and bronze objects which made the good fortune of collectors and scholars. The first incident took place on the lands of Lucien Bonaparte, the brother of Napoleon, living in Italy and made a noble by the pope with the title Prince of Canino. Lucien Bonaparte made a systematic exploration of the necropolis and set up a rich collection of which he published a brief description in 1829, entitled *Museum Etruscum*. From 1837 onwards, he placed these vases on auction in Paris. Other collections were also dispersed in these same years, and formed the core of museums such as those of Berlin, Munich, Würzburg, London, Vienna, and the Louvre.

In 1837 Stendhal concluded an article on the tombs of Corneto (Tarquinia): "I think that these tombs will be widely known within ten years."

History proved him right. It was, after all, the Etruscans and their funeral customs which made Greek vases known to us. Without the underground chambers and the practice of accumulating offerings for the dead, and without their pronounced taste for products imported from Greece, very little of this production would have reached us. In fact, in 1830 Lucien Bonaparte tried to revive the idea, which was nevertheless already out-of-date by this time, that these vases, found in Etruria, were Etruscan. He maintained that similar ones would not be found in Greece – and that was almost right, since Greece was not accessible and no systematic excavation had been undertaken there – ; he added that the fragility of the vases would prohibit all transport. In this he was mistaken. Once Greece was liberated from Ottoman rule, one could bring back vases equivalent to those discovered at Vulci, Tarquinia and elsewhere, thus confirming the Greek character of these vases, which was already indicated by a good number of inscriptions which were painted in Greek and not in Etruscan.

In these years of intensive excavation but poor attention to the nature of the contexts and the ensembles, the quantity of ceramics brought to light was prodigious. The Prussian scholar Eduard Gerhard, secretary of the *Institut de Correspondance Archéologique*, founded only a short time before in Rome (in 1828) had the great merit of understanding the importance of the event and of going to Vulci in 1831 to compile a *Rapporto Volcente* in which he described and analyzed these discoveries, thus furnishing the scholarly world with the first handbook of Greek ceramics. Filled with enthusiasm by the importance of these findings, he concluded with a beautiful flight of lyricism: "Here is but a new spring pouring out a many-faceted scholarship, which will come to water the garden of philologists and cause the progress in an extraordinary manner of artistic, archaeological and historical knowledge!"

Science must, according to him, delight in this new contribution and scholars must learn to look at these images as new historical documents, without isolating them one from another. Gerhard thus proposed this maxim to the scholars: "He who has seen but a single monument has seen nothing; he who has seen a thousand has seen one" (*Monumentorum artis qui unum vidit, nullum vidit; qui millia vidit, unum vidit*). Historical interpretation can only be founded on the study of series and the comparison of objects among themselves within each class. Gerhard, following this

logic, published the first great collection of vases, categorized according to a thematic logic using the drawings which were to be as precise as possible, putting documentary interest ahead of aesthetic quality (cf. fig. 55 and 138).

Once Greece was opened to archaeologists, from the second half of the 19th century, other series of vases and other centers of production were discovered, and the archaeologists set themselves to classifying the works according to typological criteria – in the manner of the natural sciences – Corinthian, Laconian (first called Cyrenaic), Attic, Boeotian, Chalcidian, Rhodian, etc.

It is this geographical and typological logic which dominates at the end of the 19th century, for example in the organization of the rooms of the Louvre, under the direction of the appropriately-named Edmond Pottier. The rooms followed chronological order, from the geometric of the 8th century BC to the styles of Southern Italy in the 4th century BC, grouping according to centers of production the rich collections (more than 6,000 vases) which were increased in 1863 by the block acquisition of the Campania collection, also formed in Italy.

At the beginning of his descriptive catalogue published in 1895, Pottier posed

180. WEDGWOOD VASE, FINE STONEWARE WITH SATIN SURFACE
APPROXIMATELY 1775-1790, HEIGHT 0.22 M
PARIS, CABINET DES MÉDAILLES, BIBLIOTHÈQUE NATIONAL

the question "What is the purpose of a Greek vase museum?" and gave a threefold response: The painted vases allow us to glimpse that which could be the painting of the ancient peoples, lost today. They are historical documents whose images allow us to illustrate social and cultural life in ancient times. And they are a precious chronological clue which allows us to date archaeological finds.

At the distance of a century, it would without doubt be necessary to qualify these rather optimistic responses. The chronological value of the vases remains unquestioned, and even if some have tried with various arguments to replace the outlines developed for Attic chronology, one generally sees an improvement in the dating.

The documentary value of the images is perhaps not as direct as Edmond Pottier thought; that which the painters showed is without doubt more the product of an aesthetic and ideological elaboration than the reflection of a reality that directly illustrates the life of the ancient Greeks. It is in any case what this book has tried to show.

The vases also, through their decoration, have a connection with painting. But what has been discovered since, in Italy at Paestum, at Vergina in Macedonia, or at Karaburun in Turkey, shows more differences than similarities between vases and large scale painting. On the other hand, if one confines oneself to the vases themselves, if one takes them for what they are without seeking to make them the shadow or reflection of a lost school of painting, then the graphic quality of these works, which are indeed minor, will not be without interest. In the course of this century it has furthermore been the object of fundamental research which has completely renewed our perception of ceramics, concerning both the artisans and their artistic personalities.

It was very quickly noticed that a certain number of vases were signed; for example the François Vase, which bears the name of the painter *Klitias egraphsen*, and that of the potter, *Ergotimos epoiesen*. While one could hesitate over the meaning of the verb *epoiesen*, "to make," which could designate the potter or the head of the workshop, there is no doubt about the meaning of the verb *graphein*, "to draw," which is applied to the painter.

The number of signed vases is, however, small and we know more signatures of potters than of painters. It is not enough to gather together all the signatures which have been preserved in order to account for the whole of Attic production. Very early on, certain archaeologists noticed that a given unsigned vase displayed formal similarities with another signed one: they therefore attributed the vases to Euphronios or to Douris, for example. But other anonymous pieces could have been compared in the same manner among themselves, without one being able to name their author. This attributionist method, following the path opened a half-century earlier in the field of Italian Renaissance painting by Morelli, identified groups of vases whose formal similarities in their details were such that one could attribute them to the same hand. The exercise could seem subjective but when it is conducted by a precise and trained eye, it has the advantage of suggesting enlightening comparisons. Such a task, outlined by two German archaeologists at the end of the 19th century, P. Hartwig and A. Furtwängler (the father

of the musician), was improved in a masterful way by the British scholar Sir John Beazley (1885-1970), who knew how to add perceptiveness to an untiring perseverance. Between 1910 and 1970 he laid the foundation for a classification of Attic vases, first for red-figures and then for black-figures, which remains indispensable to those who want to locate an image within the entirety of the production. Beazley did not see everything, but almost everything; he did not attribute all the vases, but he did not limit himself to masterpieces only. Minor output found a place in his catalogs.

To designate the innumerable painters which he isolated in this way, Beazley had to display an inventiveness which did not lack a strange poetry. Certain painters take their name from an inscription which appears on one of the vases in a group. Kleophrades is the name of a potter, and the Kleophrades painter is the one who decorated some of his vases (the same for the Amasis painter, the Brygos painter, and the Pistoxenos painter). Sometimes the name of the young man described as *kalos* was used, and so we have the Epidromos painter, the Antimenes painter, and the Leagros painter. Or sometimes the name of a character represented and named: the Diosphos painter, the Pholos painter, the Sappho painter, the Achilles painter, and the Pronomos painter. Sometimes a pictorial or graphic motif is used, for example by the painter of the Woolly Satyrs, the Kiss painter, and the Dokimasia painter. Other painters have modern names: drawn from a city (the Berlin

painter), a collection (the painter of Louvre G 433) or a past collector (Klügmann painter, Shuvalov painter).

These names are obviously fictitious; they are only labels useful for designating a group of images. It is important to avoid making them into artistic personalities whose biography would explain the work. If one looks upon these attributions as a mode of classification, the method has proven itself, especially through the piecing together of fragments of the same vase which were dispersed in different museums. Sometimes such pieces have been assembled after having been independently attributed to the same hand: the fitting together is then the experimental proof of the exactness of the attribution.

Beazley explained little of his process, preferring practice to theory. But his attributions are accurate, founded on attentive observation of the formal characteristics of the design. He did not limit himself to the anatomical detail of the eye or the ear, as Morelli suggested, but took into account the entire quantity of elements: the play of proportions, the construction of bodies, the relationship between the image and the vase itself, its layout and the organization of its ornamental parts. In black figures, the essence of the characteristic is incised; but the manner in which these incisions are managed is distinctive. One sets the rigor of the line of Kleitias or of the Amasis painter against the more relaxed suppleness of the Diosphos painter, for example.

In red-figures, the line is much more fluid and one observes a whole range of brush strokes: outline stripes which are quite wide and which isolate the figure on the field; sketched lines barely drawn on unfired clay for the placing of the figures; lines in relief for the drawing itself; and a thinned-out or diluted line for the anatomical details. From one painter to another the use of this range of brush strokes varies.

To understand these methods of working, we can consider one particular example, the Kleophrades painter, whose work we have deliberately favored within this thematic collection (fig. 17, 58, 85, 86, 91, 136–38, 157, 172), in order to not lose sight of the pictorial and aesthetic dimension of Attic production. Behind the unity of subjects, there exists of course a unity of painters. One cannot follow these two paths at the same time, but one is constantly sent back from one side to the other: from the painters to the themes and from the themes to the painters.

The Kleophrades painter takes his name from the potter with whom he worked; the potter signed his name specifying that he is the son of Amasis, one of the great black-figure potters. The Kleophrades painter belonged to the generation which followed the "Pioneers," the inventors of red-figure; his oldest works are similar to those of Euthymides. He often used a preliminary sketch, sometimes modifying his subject. The themes he treated were archaic, but he renewed them in the complexity of his compositions; the Naples hydria is a good example of this (fig. 85). His characters are thick-set; the eye is often very round, the pupil enlarged and the inside angle of the eye socket slightly open; the earlobe is large; the bridge of the nose and the thickness of the lips are often emphasized. The inscriptions in the earliest works lack meaning, and then are limited to a simple *kalos* or *kalos ei*, without

other specification, in the most recent works. The Kleophrades painter also painted black-figure, as on the lower zone of the funerary loutrophoros amphora in the Louvre (fig. 91), another sign of his taste for the archaic.

All these characteristics, which are difficult to describe in words, can be perceived as much by the analogy of one vase to another as by their contrast, in comparison with other painters. Attribution is always the result of a series of deductions and approximations; it cannot be automatic and one must avoid all dogmatism in this field. But within these limits, the lists of attributions proposed by Beazley and updated by his followers remain an indispensable working tool for someone who wants to orient himself within the rich ceramic production of the 6th and 5th centuries BC, which assured the fame of Athens throughout the entire Mediterranean basin.

DETAILS OF THE AMPHORA, FIGURE 58 (TOP)
AND OF THE PSYKTER, FIGURE 17 (BOTTOM)

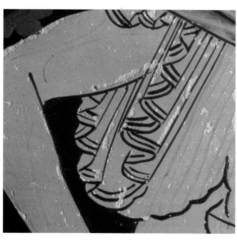

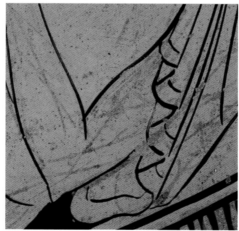

DETAILS OF THE AMPHORA, FIGURE 157 (TOP)
AND OF THE HYDRIA, FIGURE 172 (BOTTOM)

DETAILS OF THE PSYKTER, FIGURE 138 (TOP)
AND OF THE AMPHORA, FIGURE 157 (BOTTOM)

TABLE OF SHAPES

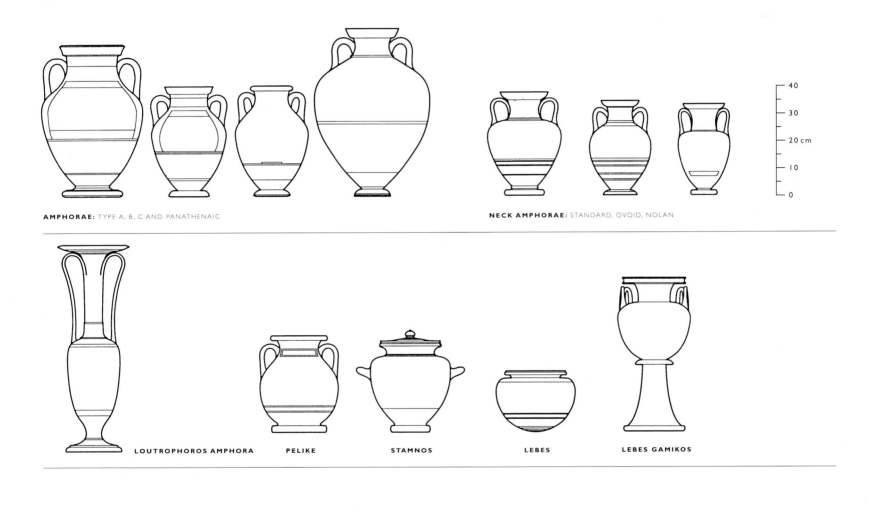

AMPHORAE: TYPE A, B, C AND PANATHENAIC

NECK AMPHORAE: STANDARD, OVOID, NOLAN

LOUTROPHOROS AMPHORA   PELIKE   STAMNOS   LEBES   LEBES GAMIKOS

KRATERS: COLUMN, CALYX, VOLUTE, BELL   PSYKTER   HYDRIA   KALPIS

OINOCHOAI: SHAPES 1, 2, 3, 7 AND 10

CUPS: COMAST, SIANA, LIP, BAND   **CUP:** TYPES A, B, AND C

KANTHAROI: TYPES A, B, AND D   **SKYPHOI:** CORINTHIAN, ATTIC   **CUP-SKYPHOS**

     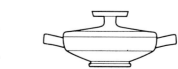

LEKYTHOI: DEIANEIRA, SHOULDER, CYLINDRICAL, SQUAT   **ARYBALLOS**   **ALABASTRON**   **PYXIS**   **LEKANE**

Aegis: clothing of Zeus or Athena, made with goat skin *(aigis),* or snake skin, and itself trimmed with snakes. Athena adds to it the head of the Gorgon as a protective element.

Agon (pl. *agones*): designates first an assembly, a reunion, but also all forms of competition, contest, struggle or proceedings.

Alabastron: small perfume vase with an oblong shape and rounded at the base.

Amphora: carrying vase with vertical handles, which is carried on both sides *(amphi-phero);* used for oil or wine.

Anodos: upward path; applies to the emergence of certain divinities from the earth.

Aoidos: singer and composer of epic poems

Aristeia: superiority *(aristos),* valor; in the Homeric epic, the moment when the poet concentrates on the particular exploits of a given hero.

Aryballos: small round-shaped perfume vase.

Astragalus: small ankle bones used for playing knucklebones

Athlon (pl. *athla*): prize of a combat or competition; the plural designates the competition or contest.

Aulos (pl. *auloi*): wind instrument similar to the oboe; usually double.

Auriga: Latin term used to designate a chariot driver, the one who holds the bit (*oreae*, "bit;" *ago*, "to hold"); in Greek, *heniochos.*

Barbiton: string instrument similar to the lyre with very long uprights.

Bema: platform which an orator or musician mounts during competitions.

Calathos: flared wicker basket for wool.

Chernips: basin containing the water for sacrificial ablutions.

Chiton: long pleated tunic, generally worn by women.

Chlamys: short cloak worn by horsemen and soldiers.

Cithara: string instrument made of tortoise shell and equipped with a large sounding board which distinguishes it from the lyre.

Cnemides: shin protectors worn by Hoplites.

Comast: participant in the *comos.*

Cronid: child of Cronos; designates, among others, Zeus.

Crotala: type of Greek castanets.

Dokimasia: a rendering of accounts by a magistrate at the end of an exercise; an examination of cavaliers and their mounts.

Ekphora: transport *(ek-phero)* of the deceased to the cemetery.

Episeme: motif placed on a shield, not simply ornamental, but with value as a symbol *(sema).*

Erastes: active subject of amorous desire *(eros);* lover.

Eromenos: object of amorous desire *(eros)*; usually younger than the erastus.

Euandria: masculine vigor; contest of male beauty.

Geranos: Greek name for the crane, it also designates the dance invented in Delos by Theseus, to celebrate the death of the Minotaur.

Gorgoneion: face of the Gorgon decapitated by Perseus; the face of terror and dread.

Harpe: sickle, agriculture instrument; often used in myth to sever heads (Gorgons, the hydra of Lerne) or to castrate Ouranos.

Hepatoscopy: examination of the liver *(hepar)* of the sacrificial victim for divinatory purposes.

Hermes: god of passages, crossroads; his name, in common speech, can designate a stone post topped with a bust. The hermes-pillar does not necessarily represent the god Hermes.

Hiera: the parts of the victim consecrated *(hieros)* to the gods; entrails.

Hieroscopy: examination of entrails *(hiera)* for divinatory purposes.

Himantes: straps of leather which boxers wrap around their fists.

Himation: rectangular cloak made of wool.

Holocaust: sacrifice where the victim is consumed by fire, and no part is eaten.

Hoplite: warrior equipped with heavy defensive armor *(hopla)*: breastplate, cnemides, helmet, round shield.

Hydria: vase used to carry water *(hydor)*; it is equipped with a vertical handle for pouring, and two horizontal handles, for lifting.

Ilioupersis: destruction of Troy (also called *Ilion*).

Ithyphallic: of the erect *(ithys)* phallus.

Kalos: beautiful (but also good).

Kanoun: sacrificial basket containing grains and the knife for slaughtering.

Kantharos: drinking vase equipped with two vertical handles, more often used by Dionysos or Herakles than by ordinary drinkers.

Kleos: renown, glory; particularly sought by epic heroes.

Kline: banquet bed, generally single; one drinks in a reclined position and not sitting up.

Kottabos: game of skill at the banquet which consists of throwing with one's cup a few drops of wine at a target while pronouncing an amorous wish.

Kouros: young man; the term was used by archaeologists to indicate a male statue without considering its function, votive or funerary, for example.

Krater: wide-mouthed vase used to mix water and wine; it is called column krater or volute krater according to its handle type, and bell krater or calyx krater according to the curvature of its belly.

Kylix: drinking cup characterized by a shallow basin and two horizontal handles.

Lebes gamikos: vase in the form of a cauldron *(lebes)* offered at the time of marriage *(gamos)*.

Lekythos: cylindrical perfume vase with a vertical handle.

Louterion: basin made of stone, mounted on a column, used for washing *(louo)*.

Loutrophoros-Amphora: long vase intended to carry *(phero)* the water for the ritual bath *(loutron),* either nuptial or funeral.

Machaira: sharp weapon with a large hooked blade; sacrificial knife.

Maenads: women who form the procession of Dionysos.

Mania: madness; applies to the Dionysian trance which seizes the maenads *(mainades)*.

Metis: crafty intelligence; the name of the goddess daughter of Okeanos, wife of Zeus; he swallowed her so not to be dethroned by his children.

Metope: element of the Doric frieze, often formed by a sculpted rectangle, between two triglyphs.

Nebris: skin of a fawn *(nebros),* in which the maenads are dressed.

Obeloi: spits used to roast meats on the flame of a sacrificial altar.

Oinochoe: jug for pouring *(cheo)* wine *(oinos)*.

Oikos: the house and the goods within it.

Omphalos: the navel; the stone which in Delphi marks the place where two eagles sent from each end of the world would meet, the center of the world.

Paideia: the education of the *pais*, the young man.

Pais (pl. *paides*): young child or all young adolescents; the term also designates a servant.

Palaestra: place where athletes train for battle *(paliaio)*.

Panathenaia: festivals in honor of Athena; the Great Panathenaia took place every four years in July. In the classical era, it is the occasion for Athens to show its political power.

Pardalis: skin of the panther *(pardalis)* often worn by maenads.

Parthenos: virgin; the term applies to Athena, the unmarried goddess.

Pelanos: ritual cake make of uncooked flour.

Pelike: type of pot-bellied amphora whose diameter is found below the height's mid-point.

Petasos: wide-brimmed flat hat work by horsemen, travelers, and hunters.

Phallophoria: transport of the *phallos* in honor of Dionysos.

Pharmakon: any substance capable of altering the nature of the body; said to be a remedy as well as a poison.

Phiale: flat cup with neither foot nor handle, used for pouring libations.

Pithos: partially buried terracotta jar with thick walls. The *pithos* serves to store grains or liquids, especially wine.

Plectrum: piece of wood or ivory used to strum the strings of the cithara.

Podanipter: bronze basin used when washing the feet of a guest.

Polos: cylindrical headgear often worn by goddesses.

Pompe: procession which escorts *(pempo)* a god or a particular group during religious festivals.

Prothesis: display of the body of the deceased.

Psykter: vase used to maintain the coolness *(psychros)* of the mixed wine which it contains; it is placed inside a krater filled with snow or ice.

Pyxis: cylindrical box; coffer.

Rhapsode: singer who performs in bringing or "stitching" together *(rhaptein)* the traditional epic songs.

Saccos: term used, perhaps incorrectly, by archaeologists to indicate female headgear, a long cone-shaped cap.

Skyphos (pl. *skyphoi*): quasi-cylindrical drinking vase with two horizontal handles, or with one vertical and one horizontal handle.

Splanchna: the main intestines (heart, lungs, liver)

Sponde (pl. *spondai*): libations in honor of the gods; in the plural it indicates an alliance or a truce which is guaranteed by the gods.

Stamnos: variety of krater with horizontal handles.

Stasis: conflict, division, civil war.

Strigil: bronze scraper used by athletes to clean themselves.

Symposiarch: master of ceremonies at the *symposion*.

Symposion: a gathering of men who drink together.

Syrinx: wind instrument made of juxtaposed reeds, a Pan flute.

Temenos: space consecrated to a divinity.

Thusia: sacrifice offered to the gods.

Thyrsus: staff decorated at one end with a bouquet of ivy; often held by the maenads, sometimes by satyrs and by Dionysos himself.

Xenia: bonds of hospitality.

Xenos: both guest and stranger, the one whom one welcomes.

87. Warsaw, National Museum 198559; ARV² 1343: May be compared with the painter of Louvre G 433

88, 89. New York, Metropolitan Museum 14.130.15; J. Boardman JHS 86 (1956) 1-5; Davison, *Attic Geometric Workshops*, p. 111: between the Villard group and the Hirschfeld group

90. Paris, Louvre CA 255; ABV 90/8: Burgon group

91. Paris, Louvre CA 453; ARV² 184/22: Kleophrades painter

92. Paris, Louvre CA 1640; D.C. Kurtz, *Athenian White Lekythoi*, Oxford, 1975, p. 203, pl. 20, 1: not attributed

93, 94. Athens, Museum of Archaeology 1958; ARV² 748/2: Inscription painter

95, 96. Athens, Museum of Archaeology 1816; ARV² 1383/12: Group R

97, 98. Paris, Louvre L 55; ARV² 924/33: Wedding painter

99. Paris, Louvre S 1671; ARV² 833: Amphitrite painter

100-102. Paris, Cabinet des Médailles 508, ARV² 1610: not attributed

103. Paris, Louvre F 384bis (CA 1961); ABL 239/135: Diosphos painter

104, 105. Vienna, Kunsthistorisches Museum 1144; ARV² 1188: imitation of the Cadmos painter

106. Paris, Louvre G 112; ARV² 117/7: Epidromos painter

107, 108. Paris, Louvre G 496; ARV² 1190/24: Pothos painter

109. Paris, Louvre G 149; ARV² 473/212: Macron

110. Paris, Cabinet des Médailles 542; ARV² 438/133: Douris

111. Vienna, Kunsthistorisches Museum 3739; ARV² 210/173: Berlin painter

112. Paris, Cabinet des Médailles 229; ABV 320/1: Three Lines group

113, 114. Vienna, Kunsthistorisches Museum 688; ARV² 255/2: Recalls the Argos painter

115, 166. Paris, Cabinet des Médailles 866; ARV² 265/80 and 1538/3: Syriskos painter

117, 118. Paris, Louvre G 192; ARV² 208/160; Berlin painter

119. Olympia, Museum of Archaeology

120. Paris, Cabinet des Médailles 811; ARV² 829/45: Stieglitz painter

121. Paris, Louvre MNB 909; ABL 235/70: Diosphos painter

122, 123. Paris, Cabinet des Médailles 397; ARV² 285/8: Geras painter

124, 125. Paris, Louvre CA 598; ABL233/19: Diosphos painter

126. Paris, Louvre F 387; ABL 238/132: Diosphos painter

127. Florence, Museum of Archaeology 4209; ABV 76/1: Clitias (cf. 1)

128, 129. New York, Metropolitan Museum 41.162.29; ABL 226/6: Sappho painter. Cf. C. Jubier-Galinier, "Héraclès, entre hommes et bêtes," in *Le bestiaire d'Héraclès*, pp. 75-85

130, 131. Paris, Cabinet des Médailles 202; A. Rumpf, *Chalkidsche Vasen*, Berlin 1927, p. 8 n° 3: Inscriptions painter

132. Paris, Louvre E 701; J. Hemelrijk, *Caeretan Hydriae*, Mainz 1984, n° 4: Painter of the Caeretan Hydriae

133. Sant'Agata dei Goti, Mustilli Collection; ARV² 1420/5: Painter of London F 64. Cf. A.F. laurens, F. Lissarrague, "Le bûcher d'Héraclès: l'empreinte du dieu," in *Entre hommes et dieux*, A.-F. Laurens, ed., Paris 1989, pp. 81-98

134. Vienna, Kunsthistorisches Museum 933; ARV² 1439/1: closely related to the Budapest group

135. Paris, Cabinet des Médailles 219; ABL 238/120: Diosphos painter (cf. 158)

136-138. Compiègne, Musée Vivenel V 1068; ARV² 188/66: Kleophrades painter

139-141. Paris, Cabinet des Médailles 444; ARV² 1112/3: Painter of Tarquinia 707

142. Olympia, Museum of Archaeology B 1975; LIMC Athena 362. E. Kunze, *Olympische Forschungen II, Archaische Schildbänder*, Berlin 1950, No X 17d, pp. 15 and 78 sq, pl. 31

143. Paris, Cabinet des Médailles 222; ABV 152/25: Amasis painter (cf. 166)

144, 145. Richmond, Virginia Museum 81.70; J. Oakley, *Antike Kunst* 30 (1987) pp. 123-130

146. Paris, Cabinet des Médailles 424; ARV² 1036/12: Hektor painter

147-149. Florence, Museum of Archaeology 70 800; ARV² 413/25: Dokimasia painter

150. Paris, Louvre F33; ABV 141/3: London B 174 group (closely related to group E)

151. Florence, Museum of Archaeology 4209; ABV 76/1: Clitias (cf. 1)

152. Paris, Cabinet des Médailles 418; ARV² 260/2: Syriskos painter

153, 154. Paris, Cabinet des Médailles 401; *LIMC* Boreas n° 17

155, 156. Paris, Cabinet des Médailles 372; ARV² 987/4: Achilles painter

157. Munich, Antikensammlung 2344; ARV² 182/6: Kleophrades painter

158. Paris, Cabinet des Médailles 219; ABV 238/120: Diosphos painter (cf. 96)

159. Paris, Cabinet des Médailles 440; ARV² 252/52: Syleus painter

160-162. Paris, Cabinet des Médailles 320; ABV 389: not attributed

163. Florence, Museum of Archaeology 4209; ARV² 76/1: Clitias (cf. 1)

164, 165. Paris, cabinet des Médailles 576; ARV² 371/14: Brygos painter

166. Paris, Cabinet des Médailles 222; ABV 152/25: Amasis painter (cf. 102)

167. Paris, Cabinet des Médailles 509; ARV² 77/91: Epictetos

168, 169. Florence, Museum of Acrhaeology 73749; ARV² 359/39: Colmar painter

170. Paris, Louvre G 144; ARV² 462/43: Macron

171. Munich, Antikensammlung 2654; ARV² 462/47: Macron

172. Rouen, Museum of Archaeology 538.3; ARV² 188/68: Kleophrades painter

173, 174. Compiègne, Musée Vivenel V 1025; ARV² 1055/76: Polygnotos group

175, 176. Florence, Museum of Archaeology 3897; T. Carpenter, *Dionysian Imagery in the Archaic Period*, pp. 89-90; *LIMC* Silenoi 120

177-179. Naples, Museum of Archaeology 3240; ARV² 1336/1: Pronomos painter

180. Paris, Cabinet des Médailles; I. Aghion, *Vrai ou Faux*, exhibition Paris 1988, n° 19, pp. 78-79. The motif is taken from Caylus, *Recueil* II, pl. 43, 3

The reader will find here, chapter by chapter, a certain number of essential bibliographical references.

FOREWORD

On Greek ceramics in general:

P.E. Arias, M. Hirmer and B.B. Shefton, *Greek History of Vase Painting,* London, 1962.

E. Simon, M. Hirmer, *Die griechischen Vasen,* 2nd ed., Munich 1981, which has not been translated.

J. Boardman, *La Céramique antique,* Paris, 1985 (original in Italian, no English edition) also deals with Egypt and the Roman world.

The most complete handbook is that of:

R.M. Cook, *Greek Painted Pottery,* London, 3rd ed., 1997.

Also see:

B. Sparkes, *Greek Pottery, an Introduction,* Manchester 1991

Ibid., *The Red and the Black, Studies in Greek Pottery,* London, 1996

I. Scheibler, *Greichische Töpferkunst,* Munich, 1983

D.J.R. Williams, *Greek Vases,* 2nd ed., London 1999

M. Denoyelle, *Chefs-d'oeuvre de la céramique greque dans les collections du Louvre,* Paris, 1994.

One finds a treatment of ceramics in most of the handbooks on the history of Greek art; one can consult in particular the account by F.Villard in the series "l'Univers des Formes:"

J. Charbonneaux, R. Martin, F. Villard, *Archaic Greek Art,* London, 1971.

Id., *Classical Greece,* London 1973.

Id., *Hellenistic Art,* London 1973.

A recent colloquium (in honor of F. Villard), *Céramique et peinture greques, modes d'emploi,* under the scientific direction of M.C. Villanueva, F. Lissarrague, P. Rouillard, A. Rouveret, Paris 1999, treats many aspects concerning ceramics, outside of the questions of iconography.

A good presentation of general problems in a volume in honor of R.M. Cook:

Looking at Greek Vases, T. Rasmussen, N. Spivey, eds. Cambridge 1991

On the technical aspects see:

J. Noble, *The Techniques of Painted Attic Pottery,* 2nd ed., London 1988.

Thematic presentation of vases: C. Bérard et al., *La cité des images,* Paris-Lausanne, 1984

M.C. Villanueva, *Images de la vie quotidienne en Grèce dans l'Antiquité,* Paris 1992.

On mythology and images:

Lexikon Iconographicum Mythologiae Classicae, Zurich-Munich, 9 vol., in progress, 1981-2000

T. Carpenter, *Art and Myth in Ancient Greece,* London, 1991

H.A. Shapiro, *Myth into Art, Poet and Painter in Classical Greece,* London 1994

I. Aghion, C. Barbillon, F. Lissarrague, *Gods and Heroes of Classical Antiquity,* Paris-New York, 1996

S. Georgoudi, J.-P. Vernant, eds., *Mythes grecs au figuré, de l'Antiquité au Baroque.* Paris 1996

A. Snograss, *Homer and the Artists, Text and Picture in Early Greek Art,* Cambridge, 1998

A special volume of the journal *Métis,* V (1990). *Autour de l'image,* is dedicated to the iconography of vases.

Also see, on painters and questions of style, the bibliography of the appendices.

PROLOGUE

On the restoration of the François vase, *Bolletino d'Arte, Serie speciale* 1, 1981

On the inscriptions, R. Wachter, *Muesum Helveticum* 48 (1991) 86-113

A. Stewart, "Stesichoros and the François Vase," in W. Moon, ed., *Ancient Greek Art and Iconography,* Madison 1983, pp. 53-74

C. Isler-Kerényi, "Der François-Krater zwischen Athen und Chiusi," in J. Oakley, W. Coulson, O. Palagia eds., *Athenian Potters and Painters,* Oxford 1997, 523-539

AT THE BANQUET

On the banquet:

J.-M. Dentzer, *Le motif du banquet couché dans le Proche-Orient et le monde grec du VIIᵉ au VIᵉ s. av J.-C.,* Paris 1982

F. Lissarrague, *The Aesthetics of the Greek Banquet,* Princeton 1987

Sympotica, O. Murray, ed., Oxford 1990

P. Schmitt, *La Cité au banquet,* Paris-Rome 1992

UNDER THE GAZE OF EROS

On seduction:

A. Greifenhagen, *Griechische Eroten,* Berlin 1957

K. Dover, *Greek Homosexuality,* London 1978

B. Calame, *L'Éros dans la Grèce antique,* Paris 1996

A. Schnapp, *Le chasseur et la Cité,* Paris 1997

On the image of women:

F. Lissarrague, "Figures of Women," in

P. Schmitt Pantel ed., *A History of Women in the West,* 1. From Ancient Goddesses to Christian Saints, Cambridge Mass. 1992, pp. 139-229.

ATHLETES, GAMES, COMPETITIONS

On the games:

E.N. Gardiner, *Athletics of the Ancient World,* Oxford 1930

R. Patrucco, *Lo sport nella Grecia antica,* Florence 1972

Le sport dans le Grèce antique; du jeu à la compétition, exhibition catalog, Palais des Beaux-Arts, Brussels, 1992

Olympism in Antiquity I; II; III, exhibition catalogues, Olympic Museum, Lausanne, respectively 1990, 1996 and 1998

On the Panathenaia:

Goddess and Polis. The Panathenaic Festival in Ancient Athens, J. Neils, ed., Princeton 1992

WARRIORS AND HEROES

On war:

P. Ducrey, *Guerre et guerriers dans la Grèce antique,* Paris 1985

F. Lissarrague, *L'autre guerrier,* Paris-Rome 1990

On the arms of Achilles:

D.J.R. Williams, "Ajax, Odysseus and the Arms of Achilles," *AntK* 23 (1980), pp. 137-145

N. Spivey, "Psephological Heroes," in *Ritual, Finance, Politics. Athenian Democratic Accounts Presented to David Lewis,* Oxford 1994, pp. 39-51

On the heroic death:

N. Loraux, *Les expériences de Tirésias, le féminin et l'homme grec,* Paris 1989 (in particular the second half, "Faiblesse de la force")

J.-P. Vernant, *Mortals and Immortals,* Princeton 1991

On the hunt:

A. Schnapp, *Le chasseur et le Cité,* Paris 1997

D. von Bothmer, *Amazons in Greek Art,* Oxford 1957 (useful repertory of images)

PASSAGES

On funerals:

G. Ahlberg, *Prothesis and Ekphora in Greek Geometric Art,* Göteborg 1971

D.C. Kurtz, J. Boardman, *Greek Burial Customs,* London 1971

E. Vermeule, *Aspects of Death in Early Greek Art and Poetry,* Berkeley 1979

H.A. Shapiro, "The Iconography of Mourning in Athenian Art," *AJA* 95 (1991), pp. 629-656

On marriage:

J. Oakley, R.H. Sinos, *The Wedding in Ancient Athens,,* Madison 1993

F. Lissarrague, "Regards sur le marriage grec," in *Silence et fureur,* O. Cavalier, ed., Avignon, Calvet museum, 1996, pp. 415-433

A.-M. Verilhac, C. Vial, *Le mariage grec, du VIe av. J.-C. à l'époque d'Auguste, BCH Supplément* 32, Paris 1999

MEN AND GODS

On libation:

F. Lissarrague, "Un rituel du vin: la libation," in *In vino verritas,* O. Murray, M. Tecusan, eds., London, 1995, pp. 126-144

On sacrifice:

M. Detienne, J.-P. Vernant et al., *The Cuisine of Sacrifice Among the Greeks,* Chicago 1989

J.-L. Durand, *Sacrifice et labour en Grèce ancienne; essai d'anthropologie religieuse,* Paris 1986

F. van Straten, *Hiera Kala; Images of Animal Sacrifice in Archaic and Classical Greece,* Leyden, 1995

M. Detienne, *Appolon le couteau à la main,* Paris 1998

On the assemblies of gods:

F. Lissarrague, A.F. Laurens, "Entre dieux," *Métis* V (1990) pp. 53-74

A HERO FOR ALL DANGERS

On Herakles the bibliography is the size of the hero. We are limited here to the education of Herakles:

C. Brillante, "La paideia di Eracle," in *Héraclès d'une rive à l'autre de la Méditerranée,* pp 199-222, Brussels-Rome, 1992

M. Schmidt, "Linos, Eracle, ed altri ragazzi. Problemi di lettura," in *Modi e funzioni del racconto mitico nella ceramica greca, italiota ed etrusca,* Salerno 1995, pp. 13-31

Three Heraklean colloquia, edited by C. Bonnet and C. Jourdain-Annequin:

Héraclès d'une rive à l'autre de la Méditerranée, Brussels-Rome 1992

Héraclès, les femmes et le féminin, Brussels-Rome 1996

Le bestiaire d'Héraclès, Kernos, supplement 7, 1998

That which is essential on the iconographic documentation is collected by J. Boardman in the article "Herakles" in *LIMC,* which contains 3520 references.

MYTHIC IDENTITY OF THE ATHENIANS

On Erichthonios:

N. Loraux, *The Children of Athena, Athenian Ideas about Citzenship and the Division between the Sexes,* Princeton 1993

N. Loraux, *Nés de la terre, mythe et politique à Athènes,* Paris 1996

On Triptolemos:

Ch. Dugas, "La mission de Triptolème d'après l'imagerie athénienne," *Recueil Dugas,* Paris 1960, pp. 123-139

G. Schwarz, *Triptolemos. Ikonographie einer Agrar- und Mysteriengottheit,* Graz 1987

On Theseus:

B. Calame, *Thésée et l'imaginaire athénien,* Lausanne 1990

DIONYSOS AND HIS FOLLOWERS

The bibliography concerning Dionysos is endless; we deal only with his iconography:

G. Hedreen, *Silens in Attic Black-Figure Vase-Painting, Myth and Performance,* Ann Arbor, 1992

T. Carpenter, *Dionysian Imagery in Archaic Greek Art,* Oxford 1986

T. Carpenter, *Dionysian Imagery in Fifth-Century Athens,* Oxford 1997

A. Schöne, *Der Thiasos, eine ikonographische Untersuchung über das Gefolge dea Dionysos in der attaschen Vasenmalerei des 6. Und 5. Jhs v. Chr.,* Göteborg 1987

F. Frontisi-Ducroux, *Le dieu masque, une figure du Dionysos d'Athènes,* Paris-Rome 1991

S. Moraw, *Die Mänade in der attischen Vasenmalerei des 6. und 5. Jhs. V. Chr.,* Mainz 1998

EPILOGUE

E. Simon, "Die *Omphale* des Demetrios. Zur Satyrspielvase in Neapel," *Archaeologischer Anzeiger* 86 (1971), pp. 199-206

C. Calame, *Le récit en Grèce ancienne,* Paris 1986, pp. 101-117

J. Winckler, in *Nothing to do with Dionysos?*, J. Winckler, F. Zeitlin eds., Princeton 1989, pp. 20-62

F. Frontisi-Ducroux, *Du masque au visage; aspects de l'identité en Grèce ancienne,* Paris 1995, pp. 41-47

F. Lissarrague, "Images dans la cité," *Métis* IX-X (1994-1995), pp. 237-244

APPENDICES

On the rediscovery of the vases:

K. Pomian, A.-F. Laurens eds., *L'anticomanie. La collection d'antiquités aux XVIIIe et XIXe siècles,* Paris 1992

I. Jenkins, K. Sloan, *Vases and Volcanoes, Sir William Hamilton and his Collection,* British Museum exhibition, London 1996

Luciano Bonaparte, le sue collezioni d'arte, le sue residenze a Roma, nel Lazio, in Italia (1804-1840), M. Natoli ed., Rome 1997

On Greek painting:

P. Moreno, *Pittura greca,* Milan 1987

I. Scheiber, *Griechische Malerei,* Munich, 1997

A. Rouveret, *Histoire et imaginaire de la peinture ancienne(V^e av. J.-C., 1er ap. J.-C.),* Paris-Rome 1989

The principal lists of attributions are those of Beazley:

J.D. Beazley, *Attic Black-Figure Vase-Painters,* Oxford 1956

J.D. Beazley, *Attic Red-Figure Vase-Painters,* 2nd ed., Oxford 1963

J.D. Beazley, *Paralipomena,* Oxford 1971

To which must be added the recent updating:

Beazley Addenda, 2nd ed., Oxford 1989 and for black-figure lekythoi:

E. Haspels, *Attic Black-Figured Lekythoi,* Paris 1936

On Beazley and his research:

D.C. Kurtz, *The Berlin Painter, Drawings by Sir John Beazley,* Oxford 1983

Ph. Rouet, *The Modern Interpretaion of Attic Vases. A comparative Study of Beazley and Pottier,* Oxford (forthcoming)

On the Kleophrades painter:

J.D. Beazley, *The Kleophrades Painter,* Mainz 1974 (original edition in German, 1933)

J. Boardman, "The Kleophrades Painter at Troy," *Antike Kunst* 19 (1976) pp. 3-18

F. Lissarrague, "Un peintre de Dionysos, le peintre de Kléophradès," in F. Berti ed., *Dionysos mito e mistero,* Commachio 1991, pp. 257-276

For a good, generously illustrated presentation by painters following the classifications by Beazley, one will refer to the handbooks of J. Boardman:

Athenian Black-Figure Vases, London 1974

Athenian Red-Figure Vases: The Archaic Period, London 1975

Athenian Red-Figure Vases: The Classical Period, London 1989

M. Robertson proposes for his part a stimulating rereading of Beazley:

The Art of Vase-Painting in Classical Athens, Cambridge 1992

Finally, we point out the series *Kerameus,* published in Mainz, which includes a dozen monographs on painters.

Photography Credits:

Aix-en-Provence, CNRS Centre Camille Jullian, Foliot85, 86 ; A. Chéné, 92. Baltimore, Johns Hopkins University, 61.

Compiègne, Antoine Vivenel Museum, Christian Schryve, 136, 138, 173.

Florence, Soprintendenza Archeologica della Toscana, 1, 2, 3, 4, 6, 8, 12, 74, 127, 163.

New York, The Metropolitan Museum of Art, Rogers Fund 1914, 89, 128.

Paris, Artephot, André Held, 93, 96.

Paris, François Lissarrague, 178.

Paris, Magnum, Erich Lessing, 23, 26, 33, 34, 35, 36, 50, 53, 54, 58, 60, 64, 65, 69, 71, 72, 73, 75, 76, 77, 78, 81, 82, 83, 87, 90, 91, 98, 99, 103, 104, 105, 106, 107, 108, 109, 111, 113, 114, 117, 120, 125, 126, 132, 134, 150, 157, 171.

Paris, Stefano Bianchetti, 9, 14, 15, 16, 18, 20,21, 22,24,25,28, 29,31,32,38,39,40, 41, 42, 43, 44, 62, 63, 66, 67, 68, 79, 80, 101, 102, 110, 112, 115, 116, 120, 122, 123, 130, 135, 139, 143, 146, 149, 152, 153, 154, 155, 156, 158, 159, 160, 161, 162, 164, 165, 167, 168, 174, 175, 179.

Princeton, The Art Museum of Fine Arts, Katherine Wetzel, 144, 145.

Rouen, Departmental Museum of the Antiquities, Yohann Desiandes, 172.

The other photographs come from the collection of Éditions Hazan.

Source of drawings:

A. Furtwängler, K. Reichhold, *Griechische Vasenmaleri,* 4 5, 7, 11, 13, 151

A. de Ridder, *Catalogue de Vases peints de la Bibliothèque nationale,* 27, 37, 141

E. Gerhard, *Auserlesene Vasenbilder,* 55, 137

G. Rodenwaldt *Olympia,* 119

Duc de Lynes, *Description de quelques vases peints,* 131

E. Kunze, *Archaïsche Schilbänder,* 142

B. Sparkes, *Greek Pottery,* pp. 226-227

All other drawings are by the author.

©1999, Éditions Hazan

Graphic conception and production: Thierry Dubreil
Coordination: Juliette Hazan

Iconographic research: Juliette Charlot
Photographic campaign: Stefano Bianchetti
Manufacture: Frédérique Cadoret

Printing: EuroGrafica Spa, Marano Vicenza

English translation © 2001 Riverside Book Company, Inc.
Translation by Kim Allen
Edited by Brian Eskenazi

Printed in Italy
ISBN: 1-878351-57-5